ACADEMIC LANGUAGE
Assessment and Development of Individual Needs

Second Edition
A. L. A. D. I. N.
Book One

Lessons 1–3

Pretest 1 and Posttest 1

Phyllis Kuehn

Pearson
Custom
Publishing

PEARSON CUSTOM PUBLISHING
75 Arlington Street, Suite 300, Boston, MA 02116
A Pearson Education Company

To the Students

Welcome to ALADIN. This program will help you develop the language skills you need to be a success in college. Your language skills continue to develop your entire life. This curriculum will give you the tools to continue this language development for a particular kind of specialized language – academic language.

All of you speak English, but spoken English can be very different from the academic language of the college lecture and the college textbook. After doing research on academic language for a number of years, I was able to determine what kinds of language skills students need to be prepared for the college classroom. Your level of academic language is directly related to your academic success.

Hundreds of students have already used this curriculum and have reported success in developing their language skills. You will have the same success as you go through this book. You can see the work and comments of some students who have already experienced ALADIN by visiting the ALADIN web site at www.academic-language.com. If you want to contribute some work or comments to this web site, send us an email or ask your teacher to contact ALADIN. We want to hear from you!

To the Instructors

The video tapes and Instructor's Guide that go with this book are available through the ALADIN web site at www.academic-language.com. If you have suggestions for the book or would like to post messages to your students, assignments, or student work on the web site, please contact us there. We can also put a link to your institution's web page on the ALADIN web site. The ALADIN web site also has useful links for students to information and research web pages they can use for assignments.

Acknowledgments

This assessment and curriculum were developed with support from the Fund for the Improvement of Postsecondary Education (FIPSE), U.S. Department of Education. The effectiveness of the program was documented under a second grant from FIPSE that supported wide dissemination of the materials. Without these grants, the assessment and curriculum could not have been developed. The commitment of the program officers at FIPSE to support projects that provide meaningful access to students in postsecondary education continues to be an important element of educational equity and improvement in the United States.

College faculty members who developed the half-hour lectures that form the basis of each lesson proved that a good teacher can teach well under any circumstances. The professors selected for this project were identified by students and faculty across campus as outstanding lecturers. Their willingness to participate in this project by providing the lectures and suggesting supplementary text materials is gratefully acknowledged. Many thanks to Dr. David Tanner, Dr. Reuben Sanchez, and Dr. Ida Jones.

The instructors who have used these materials have provided several of the lesson ideas and have helped with revisions over the years of development. Gena Rice has contributed to both the research that supported the assessment development and to several elements in the lessons. Carol Goiburn, the first teacher to adopt the program and use it with her high school students, has also served as a mentor to other teachers. Ideas and suggestions have also been contributed by Jenny Cobb, Lesa Schwartz, Binbin Jiang, and Dean Christensen. I am grateful for their help.

Phyllis Kuehn
Clovis, California

ALADIN BOOK 1 TABLE OF CONTENTS

I.   Lesson 1   The Pretest Revisited 1
Educational Psychology Lecture
Dr. David Tanner

        Lesson 1 Dictionary 43

II.   Lesson 2   English Literature Lecture 57
Dr. Reuben Sanchez

        Lesson 2 Dictionary 103

III.   Lesson 3   The Legal System 119
Dr. Ida Jones

        Lesson 3 Dictionary 153

IV.   Your Blank Dictionary   Appendix 1

V.   Pretest   Appendix 2

IV.   Posttest   Appendix 3

Academic **L**anguage: **A**ssessment and **D**evelopment of **I**ndividual **N**eeds

LADIN

LESSON 1

ALADIN Lesson 1   Table of Contents

Table of Contents   2

1. Lecture Signals, Note-taking Strategies   3

        Lecture Signals   4
        Symbols, Abbreviations   7
        Pretest Model Lecture Notes   11
        Note-taking Again   14
        Lecture Question Model Answer   16

2. Academic Vocabulary Building   17

        Word Attack Skills   18
        Word Forms   20
        Word Parts: Prefixes, Suffixes, Roots 23
        Reading Word Attack Skills   27
        Reading Sentence Completion   30

3. Reading Skills and Strategies; Note-taking   32
    And Summarizing
        Reading Underlining   32
        Summarizing Strategies   34
        Reading Note-taking   38

4. Sentence Complexity   40

5. Academic Culture   42

Dictionary Lesson 1   43

ALADIN Internet Site

www.academic-language.com

Using the Test Results: The First Lesson

The first lesson in this curriculum begins with the test results of your pretest of academic language proficiency.

You will see your profile of scores and be able to compare how you did with how other students did on this test. Then you will be doing a lesson designed to develop academic language skills -- the language skills you need to be a successful college student. In this lesson and in each lesson of the ALADIN curriculum you will be developing the following:

- lecture and reading note-taking skills
- academic vocabulary and phrases
- reading strategies
- ability to understand the most common kinds of complex sentences found in academic lectures and textbooks
- knowledge of academic culture

Like the test you took, each lesson is based on a videotaped lecture and readings from college textbooks.

_____

Lecture Signals, Note-Taking Strategies, Abbreviations, and Tricks Used by Good Note-Takers

Students who take good lecture notes do not try to write down everything the professor is saying. The eleven minutes of Dr. Tanner's lecture you listened to and took notes on contained 1,745 words, or approximately 160 words per minute! Good students know that not everything the professor says is of equal importance. They listen for cues or signals from the professor that indicate what is important to write down. When they take notes, good students use abbreviations, symbols, and other tricks to make their note-taking easier and more efficient.

In this lesson we will begin to study the signals professors use to indicate the importance of what they are saying. We will also learn a variety of abbreviations and symbols students use in their notes.

Why are good lecture notes important?

Research shows that in high school, the teacher generally **leads** students **into** the textbook. That is, the teacher provides help so the students understand the information presented in the textbook. In college, the professor usually assumes that you have already read and understood the assigned textbook reading and he or she will be providing new information or expanding on the information in the textbook. In other words, the professor is not usually just repeating what is in the textbook. You will need good lecture notes as a source of this new information. You may need to answer test questions by integrating or putting together information from the textbook with information from the lecture. Good notes will help you study for the tests. The information that the professor emphasized in the lecture is probably what he or she will consider important for the test.

What do good note-takers do?

1. They don't try to write down everything the professor says.
2. They don't try to write down complete sentences.
3. They restate and summarize what the professor says by using their own words as well as the words used by the professor.
4. They use symbols and abbreviations for common words and relationships.
5. They have a structure to their notes that follows the structure of the lecture. Each new piece of information is separated from previous information. Examples are labeled as examples.
6. They are able to understand the signals the professor uses to give structure to the information being presented.
7. If they don't understand something, they write down the information as well as they can and then put a question mark beside it as a reminder to ask the professor or to look up the information in the textbook.

Lecture Signals:

Learning the signals professors use to tell you what they consider important can help you take better lecture notes. However, the best way to take good notes and to understand what the professor considers important (and therefore what will likely be on the test) is to read the chapter in your textbook that is related to the lecture BEFORE the lecture. Even brief skimming of the textbook chapter before the lecture will give you a mental idea (schema) for the information from the lecture and some familiarity with the new vocabulary you will be hearing. Reading ahead in the textbook is the best way to make the lecture easier to understand.

Lectures always have a particular organization. Like a story, they have a beginning, a middle, and an end. Lecture signals tell you what the beginning, the middle and the end are and what's important for you to know from the lecture. You will also study some of these signals (words and phrases) in the vocabulary section of this lesson.

Lecture Signals

Signal Category	Explanation	Example
I. Topic Marker	tells you what the topic is	Today's lecture is on... The next issue we will discuss is...
II. Checkpoint Marker	**Tells you where the professor is in a lecture or when the professor is changing to a new topic or concluding the lecture.**	
A. Topic Shifter	may be an aside - almost spoken to himself/herself at the end of a particular point	Now... OK.... Let's see... Right... Alright...
B. Concluder	signals end of topic or end of lecture	That's what you need to know about... That covers the topic of...

III. Information Expander	These are important signals that give the following kinds of information:	
A. Give background information	gives the historical or social context	As you may remember from history... During this time period we also saw...
B. Explain meaning	gives a definition or restatement of the topic or idea	In other words... By this I mean...
C. Give an example	could also be anecdote (little personal story) or joke	For example... In the real world this would be... In terms of...
D. Relate two pieces of information:	**Often uses "Connector" words and phrases. (see vocabulary section)**	
1. Cause-effect	how "A" causes "B" to happen	The result of this is... This causes the following to happen...
2. Contrast	how are "A" and "B" different	In contrast... On the other hand... The opposite is true for...
3. Compare	how are "A" and "B" the same	All three men believe... Similarly...
IV. Information Qualifier	**Gives a different value to the information.**	
A. Emphasize importance of information	draws your attention to the important points in the lecture	repetition, restatement
1. Rhetorical question*	a question asked of the whole class - no answer is expected	What do you think he did next? What do you think the answer is?
2. Imperative*	an "order" to the students	Remember this. Write this down.
3. Direct statement of importance	the professor tells you directly how important something is	This is important. Pay particular attention to this point.
B. Information Corrector	professor made a mistake and is correcting himself/herself	Oh, what I meant to say was...
C. Emphasize information is not very important	extra information you don't have to write down - added to make the lecture more interesting	This may not be relevant but... By the way...
V. Summarizer	professor will summarize or restate the important information	In summary...As I said before... In other words...

* **rhetorical question** - When someone asks a rhetorical question, he or she expects no answer. It is just a question that guides the lecture or conversation. For example, when you are driving, you may ask about a driver in front of you, "What is that crazy guy doing?" You really don't expect anyone in the car to answer this rhetorical question.

* **imperative sentence** - This kind of sentence is like an order. You are telling someone what to do. The sentence usually starts with a verb: Bring me the book. Open the window. The professor is telling you to focus your attention on something: Consider the following.

LECTURE SIGNALS - Examples from Dr. Tanner's lecture.

➜ **Task:**   Work in groups to be sure you understand the meaning of each lecture signal example from Dr. Tanner's lecture.

Dr. Tanner said:	Lecture Signal:	Meaning:
1. Today's lecture is on an element of learning theory.	*I. Topic Marker*	the topic is only <u>part of</u> learning theory
2. Now I'd like to provide for you a little bit of context for the lecture as follows.	*III. Information Expander* A. Background	background information for main topic comes next
3. If one cares to look at learning theory, one will find that there are really two approaches...	*III. Information Expander* A. Background	learning theory has two parts; this topic is one part
4. Right. OK. Alright. Now.	*II. Checkpoint Marker* A. Topic Shifter	professor finished making a point and will move on to next point
5. ... they made an assumption that is very important. ... his explanation is a profoundly important one. ...the essential elements are...	*IV. Information Qualifier* A. Importance 3. Direct statement	the professor is telling you this is very important WRITE IT DOWN!
6. How does it happen that even before the animal can smell the food he has this response? What if you choose to do what I do and teach people?	*IV. Information Qualifier* A. Importance 1. Rhetorical question	the professor is not really asking you a question - just telling you that this question and its answer are important information
7. Consider the following. Now consider the situation. Remember that unconditioned descriptive means...	*IV. Information Qualifier* A. Importance 2. Imperative	the professor is trying to focus your attention on the information
8. Now you remember as I began I mentioned to you...	*V. Summarizer*	the professor is summarizing earlier information - it must be important to the current topic or new topic
9. ... his field was physiology and in fact, he won a Nobel Prize...	*III. Information Expander* A. Background	the professor gives background or related information
10. The unconditioned, or the conditioned, excuse me, the conditioned response...	*IV. Information Qualifier* B. Corrector	professors sometimes make mistakes and correct themselves - be sure you correct your notes

Symbols, Abbreviations, and Other Note-taking Tricks

You will develop your own system of note-taking as you take more college classes. You may already use some abbreviations and symbols when you take notes. However, you may want to learn and use the following methods that other students use to help you take notes from reading and lectures. The abbreviations and symbols in this lesson work equally well for lecture notes and for reading notes.

Generic Abbreviations

Abbreviation	Meaning	Abbreviation	Meaning
1. aka	also known as, alias	25. HW	homework
2. assn	association	26. ie	that is
3. asst	assistant, assist	27. imp	important
4. ave, avg	average	28. info	information
5. bldg	building	29. inc	include, including
6. cf	compare	30. lab	laboratory
7. ch	chapter	31. lang	language
8. dept	department	32. min	minimum
9. dif	different, difference	33. max	maximum
10. econ	economics	34. mid	middle
11. ed	editor; edition; education	35. misc	miscellaneous
12. et al	and others, and the others	36. n, no	number
13. etc	etcetera, and so forth, and the rest	37. neg	negative
14. esp	especially	38. na, n/a	not applicable
15. eg	for example	39. nb	pay attention, note well (nota bene)
16. ex	example	40. p, pp, pg	page
17. fig	figure	41. pop	population, popular
18. freq	frequent, frequently	42. prep	prepare, preparatory
19. ff	following	43. stu	student
20. fwd	forward	44. temp	temperature, temporary
21. gov, govt	government	45. thru	through
22. grad	graduate	46. vs, v	versus
23. gpa	grade point average	47. w, w/	with
24. H	hypothesis	48. w/out, w/o	without

Symbols

Symbol	Meaning	Symbol	Meaning
©	copyright	∧	insert
...	words missing or deleted here	℞	drugs, medicine
@	at	$	money, dollars
&	and	¶	paragraph

Math and Science Symbols

Symbol	Meaning	Symbol	Meaning
4	for	~	approximately, about the same as
K	thousand	≅	approximately equal to
+	and	≠	not equal to
=	equal, the same as, consists of	∴	therefore
±	more or less, plus or minus	∵	because
∞	infinity, infinite	>	greater than
#	number	<	less than
Ψ	psy, psychology	↑	increasing, increases
♀	female	↓	decreasing, decreases
♂	male	→	leads to, results in, is related to
%	percent	←	is a result of, comes from

New Abbreviations for Each Class, Each Lecture: Make your own abbreviations as you need them. If a word is repeated often, use an abbreviation or just one letter to represent it. For example, in Dr. Tanner's lecture, behaviorism, behavioristic, behaviorists could be abbreviated with behav, B or B-ists. In the eleven minutes of lecture you watched, Dr. Tanner said the following:

Word	Frequency	Suggested Abbreviations
learning, learn, learned, learner	22	L or Lrn
behaviorist(s), behavior	12	B-ists, B

unconditioned	14	U, Unc
stimulus, stimuli	14	S, Stim
observable, observe, observation	4	Obs
Pavlov (or "he", referring to Pavlov)	21	P

Practice 1

➜ **Task:** Think about the meaning of the following notes from the reading and lecture. Then write a complete sentence that reflects the meaning of the notes below the abbreviated information.

1. P's lab = res team

1. _____

2. UR - eg dogs sal w/o food present

2. _____

3. B-ists res → new lrn theory

3. _____

4. kids hungry ∴ dis sci

4. _____

5. res done ~ 100 yrs ago

5. _____

Practice 2

➜ **Task:** Work in groups of two or three to take notes on the following sentences. Practice using the abbreviations and symbols you are studying.

1. Pavlov spent approximately two years working on his learning theory.

_____

2. Therefore, he used male and female dogs in his experiments.

_____

3. In psychology, the influence of behaviorism is greater than the influence of cognitivism.

_____

4. Pavlov's research was considered important and lead to important changes in the way scientists viewed learning.

_____

_____

5. His theory of learning was not the same as the cognitivists' theory.

_____

Practice 3

➜ **Task:** Work in small groups to develop a list of abbreviations and symbols you might use that are not included on these lists. Present these abbreviations and symbols to the class.

Abbrev./ Symbol	Meaning	Abbrev./ Symbol	Meaning

Practice 4

➜ **Task:** Write an abbreviation or symbol for each of the following words or phrases.

Abbrev./ Symbol	Meaning	Abbrev./ Symbol	Meaning
	and so forth		hypothesis
	without		greater than
	less than		not equal
	page		leads to, results in
	therefore		paragraph
	and others		because
	also known as		insert
	forward		not applicable
	at		approximately
	female		with
	grade point average		frequent
	approximately equal to		equal, the same as

Practice 5

➜ **Task:** Work with a partner or the whole class to go over the model lecture notes on the next page. These are the notes a good note-taker took from Dr. Tanner's lecture. Try to understand the meaning of each part of the model notes and compare the model notes to your notes and your partner's notes.

Pretest Model Lecture Notes

Tanner

lecture = learning theory

ed psych - only 100 yrs - research

learning theory - 2 approaches

$\downarrow$

behaviorists - focus on observable learning

def. of learning = change in behav. -

but change not from age,
fatigue, drugs etc

imp. assumption =
universal laws of learning =
apply to all people + all animals

$\downarrow$

works for humans + animals

assum. - not prove = not emp. validate this

Pavlov - (Russ.) - theory = class. cond.

[physiology = field -
Nobel Prize]

12

P. - meas. sal. secretions - dogs
  when food → dogs sal.
  ring bell before food - then food → sal.
  then bell - no food → dog sal. anyhow

(overhead)
                    food   sal.
pair these -   US ------------> UR = means response isn't
then get   stimulus   learned   =
same   vis??(look up)
response
w/ bell   CS -----------> CR
only   bell   sal.

 application to learners - hungry stus, sci before lunch -
(overhead)
                 no food   discomfort
                  US ----------------> UR
paired }
                  CS ----------------> CR
                  sci.   disc.
            <u>doesn't</u> have to be a rational relationship

Tanner - personal example - dislikes wind chimes -
       doesn't know why - makes sad   ?? melan...
       prob. classical cond.   (look up)
       from early childhood

Practice 6

➜ **Task:**   Use the blank paper provided below to take notes from Dr. Tanner's lecture again.
REMEMBER: As you practice taking notes from the videotaped lecture, be sure to use note-taking symbols and abbreviations.

Lecture Notes: Lesson 1 Dr. Tanner - Repeat

Practice 7   Note-taking Revisited

➡ **Task:**   Work with a partner to compare your new notes to your old notes. How have your notes improved?

Improvements in My Notes: Second Time

_____

_____

_____

_____

_____

_____

Practice 8   Review of the model lecture question.

➡ **Task:**   Work with a partner to compare your lecture question answer to the model answer.

•   What information is missing from your answer?

•   What unimportant information or wrong information is included in your answer?

Model Answer for Pretest Lecture Notes Question

What was the unconditioned response in Pavlov's experiment? Why was it called unconditioned?

In Pavlov's experiment, the unconditioned response was salivation. It was considered unconditioned because the animal didn't learn to salivate. In other words, salivation was unlearned or automatic.

2. Academic Vocabulary Building

What is academic vocabulary?

In this lesson and in the lessons that follow, you will be developing your academic vocabulary. This kind of vocabulary is not commonly used in conversation -- it is used in textbooks and by professors when they teach. The words are not technical vocabulary from a particular field of study but are words used in textbooks and by professors from <u>all</u> the college fields to <u>explain</u> the technical information.

Why is vocabulary important for me to learn?

If you don't know these academic words and expressions, you will have a very hard time reading the textbooks and understanding the professor! The more vocabulary you know, the better you will be able to read, understand lectures, write, and speak. Vocabulary knowledge is the single best predictor of both reading comprehension skill and intelligence.

Learning Academic Vocabulary

Each academic vocabulary section of the lesson has two parts. First, you will study those words and phrases you have heard in the lecture or read in the reading. It is not useful to try to memorize lists of new words. This is not how we increase our vocabulary. You will study the new words in the context of the lecture and reading materials. The vocabulary will be presented in word networks because this is a useful way to remember the new words. Each network has a symbol or icon associated with it to help you remember the words. When you learn each word, you will also learn its different forms so that you will be able to understand it and use it in a variety of ways. For example, if you learn a new word like *stimulus*, which is a noun, you will also learn the verb form (stimulate), and any other forms that exist. By learning words in this way, your vocabulary and your reading and listening ability will increase rapidly.

The second part of the academic vocabulary will teach you about word parts -- prefixes, suffixes, and roots. The more you know about these word parts, the easier it is for you to guess the meaning of a new word the first time you see it or hear it. These word parts are like clues to the meaning.

Dictionary Lesson 1

Each lesson has its own dictionary arranged in the eleven vocabulary networks. Turn to the Lesson 1 Dictionary (page 43) and look at the eleven networks. The academic vocabulary words are arranged in networks related to:

1. Thinking
2. Person Characteristics
3. Importance
4. Information
5. Research, Academic
6. Cause-Effect, Change
7. Hedge, Qualify (hedge means saying something in a less direct way or in weaker way)
8. History, Government, Society

9. Time
10. Connectors and Comparisons
11. Evaluation Description

Dictionary Symbols

✔ Check it out! This symbol beside a word or phrase means that it is a "Trick Word." The way professors use this word or phrase is different from the way you commonly use the word in everyday speech. In other words, this word can trick you! It may not mean what you think it means!

✂ This symbol beside a word means that there is a prefix, root, or suffix that can help you understand the word meaning. You can cut the word apart and guess at the meaning based on the parts of the word.

Within each vocabulary network, words are arranged alphabetically. *Some words have been placed in more than one category.* Each vocabulary entry in the dictionary also includes all parts of the word that are related to its academic meaning in this lesson, a simple definition of the word, and an example sentence of how the word was used in the lecture or the reading. At the end of this book there is also a blank dictionary. You can add new words to your own dictionary as you find them in your reading in other classes. You decide which category they belong in.

Word Attack Skills

What should you do when you hear a word you don't know?

Lecture: During a lecture, you may not have time to try to decode a new word you don't know. Good students say you should do the following:

*1. **BEFORE*** the lecture, be sure to read through the textbook chapter related to the lecture topic. Make a list of the important content words and their meanings so that when you hear them in the lecture, they are familiar. For example, if you had read the book before Dr. Tanner's lecture, you would have had words like cognition, behaviorism, salivation, and stimulus on your list.

*2. **DURING*** the lecture, if you hear a word you don't know, try to write it down the way it sounds so you can look it up later. Put a question mark by the word so you remember to look it up. In the model notes, the person taking the notes did not recognize the words **visceral** and **melancholy**. In this case, the student wrote

vis ??   and   melan ??

because he or she did not know the word. This gives the student some information to use to look up the word later.

Other Strategies:

A. Listen carefully. Professors want you to understand what they are saying. When they use an unusual word like visceral or melancholy, they often restate or define the word before they use it again. Dr. Tanner did this as follows:

"He said it's visceral. It's part of the animal's being. It's not a learned behavior at all. If I come close to you and blow in your eye, you blink. And that isn't a learned response. It is something that is part of your being. ... The dog doesn't learn to salivate. It does that automatically. It is a visceral response."

As you can see, Dr. Tanner spent a lot of time explaining what he meant by visceral. So by listening carefully, you can often learn the meaning of the word from the professor's explanation.

When he was speaking about windchimes, Dr. Tanner said,

"They fill me with a sense of melancholy. And I don't know how to explain that except in terms of classical conditioning. ...And so when I hear them I feel a sense of sadness or melancholy."

Practice 9

➜ **Task:**   Work in groups of two or three to write a definition of the words visceral and melancholy based on the information Dr. Tanner gave you about these words.

1. **visceral**

2. **melancholy**

B. Ask the professor to write the unknown word on the board.

Professors want you to understand their lectures and learn the course content. They are usually willing to write important words on the board so you can copy them down. Many professors do this routinely during their lectures. Some need to be asked or reminded to write new words on the board.

You can't interrupt the professor every time you hear a word you don't know. However, if the word seems very important to the topic of the lecture, ask the professor to write the word on the board and explain it.

C. Study the vocabulary lessons in this book!

These lessons are carefully developed to teach you the academic vocabulary and phrases professors use to explain their course material. The more time you spend learning the academic vocabulary, the better your lecture comprehension and reading comprehension will be.

3. AFTER the lecture, look up any words you did not know. Don't just put your notes away until the next class. Use the textbook, the dictionary, and your friends' notes to make sure that you have good, complete notes for every lecture. When it is time to study for the midterm exam, you can spend your time learning rather than trying to make sense out of your notes. **Correcting and completing your notes after every lecture is an excellent study strategy.**

Word Forms

Most of the words you will study in these lessons (with the exception of the connectors) will have several forms, **depending on how the word is used in the sentence**. The word forms are very generally defined as:

Word Form	Definition	Example from this Lecture
Noun	a person, place, thing, or idea	professor, theory, Russia
Pronoun	takes the place of a noun	I, he, she, it, we, they, you, etc.
Verb	shows an action or a state of being	run, think, be, can, have
Adjective	usually describes a noun	rational, mental, cognitive
Adverb	usually describes a verb or adjective	irrationally, profoundly, theoretically
Connector	in these lessons, this category of words and phrases connects parts of a sentence or two sentences together in the lesson	hence, in other words, and, or, but, in contrast to, however, accordingly

During each lesson you will become more familiar with all forms of the words you study. You will learn to recognize what the word forms are through looking for cues in the word and sentence. When you come to a word you don't know in the reading or the lecture, the ability to recognize what form the word is (noun, verb, adjective, adverb) can be a big help in guessing the meaning of the word.

Practice 10   Vocabulary Word Form Practice

→ **TASK:**   Work individually or in small groups to complete the following exercise. The words below are shown in their noun form. You should list any other forms of the word that there are and try to make a sentence with any form of the word. Also find which network(s) the noun is in. Use the Lesson 1 Dictionary to check your answers. Discuss the answers in small groups or as a whole-class exercise.

	Noun	Verb?	Adjective?	Adverb?	Network?

1. perception _____

Sentence: _____

_____

2. evaluation _____

Sentence: _____

_____

3. discipline _____

Sentence: _____

_____

4. acquisition _____

Sentence: _____

_____

5. modification _____

Sentence: _____

_____

6. emphasis _____

Sentence: _____

_____

7. maturation _____

Sentence: _____

_____

8. consistency _____

Sentence: _____

_____

Noun	Verb?	Adjective?	Adverb?	Network?

9. capacity _____

Sentence: _____

_____

10. frequency _____

Sentence: _____

_____

11. theory _____

Sentence: _____

_____

12. strategy _____

Sentence: _____

_____

13. restriction _____

Sentence: _____

_____

14. conclusion _____

Sentence: _____

_____

15. motivation _____

Sentence: _____

_____

Practice 11   Using the academic vocabulary.

➡ **TASK:**   The following are adjective forms of words in Dr. Tanner's lecture and text. Work in pairs or small groups to think of a new noun that can be used with each adjective. The nouns do not have to be words from the lesson. The answers can be silly or funny as long as they make sense.

Example: *adjective* excellent + *noun* student = excellent student

Adjective +	Noun	Adjective +	Noun
1. illogical	_____	11. classical	_____
2. valid	_____	12. previous	_____
3. influential	_____	13. predictable	_____
4. fundamental	_____	14. observable	_____
5. primary	_____	15. external	_____
6. essential	_____	16. related	_____
7. symbolic	_____	17. consistent	_____
8. explicit	_____	18. relevant	_____
9. logical	_____	19. profound	_____
10. motivated	_____	20. recognizable	_____

Word Parts

PREFIXES ✚ ROOTS ✚ SUFFIXES

Learning the parts of words can <u>sometimes</u> help you guess the meaning of new words you hear and read.   You will be learning about common PREFIXES, or parts that attach to the beginning of a word, ROOTS, parts of the word that are used to build other words with similar meanings, and SUFFIXES, parts that attach to the end of words to give important hints to the meaning.

For example:

Part	Form	Meaning	Examples
Prefix	in-	not	**in**capable, **in**sane, **in**sincere
Root	-cogn-	know	**cogn**ition, **cogn**izant, in**cogn**ito **cogn**ate
Suffix	-er, -or	person who does it	teach**er**, advis**or**

Noun Suffixes

Academic language uses more nouns than we normally use in everyday speech. You can recognize many words as nouns by becoming familiar with the endings (suffixes) that are used for nouns.

Some noun endings have specific meanings and some just signal that the word is a noun but don't add any special meaning to the word.

Noun endings from Dr. Tanner's lecture and reading:

Suffix	Meaning	Example
-ism	indicates belief in some way of thinking	behavior**ism** cognitiv**ism**
-tion **-sion**	indicates noun form	assump**tion** cogni**tion** presump**tion** conclu**sion**
-ist	indicates the person who specializes in something	theor**ist** behavior**ist**
-ty	indicates noun form	universali**ty** profundi**ty**
-bility	something that can be done	capabil**ity**
-ology	the study of something	psych**ology** physi**ology**
-ance **-ence**	indicates noun form	consequ**ence** influ**ence**
-ness	indicates noun form	sad**ness**

Other Common Suffixes That Indicate Noun Form:

Noun Suffix	Example
-acity	capacity
-dom	freedom
-ery	surgery
-hood	childhood, neighborhood
-ment	government, department
-ship	penmanship, sportsmanship
-tude	attitude, altitude

Other prefixes and suffixes in Dr. Tanner's lecture and reading:

Prefix	Meaning	Example
pre-	before	presume, preexisting
re-	do again	recognize, restriction
con-	together, with	consequence
dis-	negative, not	discomfort
un-	negative, not	unconditioned
in, ir, il, im	negative, not	inexperience, irrational, illogical, immature

Suffix	Meaning	Example
-ize	verb ending	recognize
-ed	past verb or adjective	He *called* (verb) the stimulus a *conditioned* (adjective) stimulus.
-able	adjective ending, can be done	observable
-ful	adjective ending, full of	youthful, meaningful
-al; -ar	adjective endings	rational, visceral; universal
-ive; -ic	adjective endings	perceptive, cognitive; symbolic

Roots found in Dr. Tanner's lecture and reading

Root	Meaning	Example
cogn	know	cognition, metacognition, recognize
matur	ripe, grown	maturation
psyche	mind, soul	psychology
physis	nature	physiology
sequ	follow	sequence, consequence
sume, sumpt	take, take up	assume, presume, resume, subsume
dic, dict	say	dictation, predict, contradict
logos	reason, word	logical, illogically

Verb Endings

-ed	past tense	he learned
-ing	continuing action	he is learning*
-s	present tense with he, she, or it	he learns

* -ing can also sometimes indicate a noun
   for example - Swimming is fun. (noun=swimming)
  -ize is a common verb ending: economize, alphabetize
  -ate is another common verb ending: originate, complicate, abbreviate

Adverbs

Adverbs are most often formed by adding some form of **-ly, -ily, -ally** to the adjective form of the word, unless the adjective already has a -y ending. Examples from Dr. Tanner's lecture and reading:

Adjective	Adverb	Context: Dr. Tanner Said
frequent	frequently	The formal definition of learning goes **frequently** something like this:
profound	profoundly	His explanation of learning is a **profoundly** important one.
illogical	illogically	I somehow **illogically** associate something with wind-chimes.
observable	observably	Their behaviors after instruction are **observably** different.

Practice 12 Using roots, prefixes, and suffixes to guess word meaning.

➜ **Task:** Use the prefix, suffix, and root information to explain the following words and indicate what form (noun, verb, adjective, adverb) of the word they are. Work in small groups.

Word	Form?	Prefix, root, suffix?	Meaning
1. unrecognizable	_____	_____	
2. illogically	_____	_____	
3. presumption	_____	_____	
4. prediction	_____	_____	
5. consequences	_____	_____	
6. recognized	_____	_____	
7. psychology	_____	_____	
8. maturation	_____	_____	
9. youthful	_____	_____	
10. behaviorist	_____	_____	

Reading Word Attack Skills:

When you are reading and come to a word you don't know, use the following word attack methods to try to guess the meaning of the new word. First ask yourself questions about the word and what is around it. Then, guess the meaning of the word.

Example: It is the individual's **preexisting** network of concepts, strategies, and understanding that makes experience meaningful.

Step	Question: PREEXISTING	Answer
1	Are there any prefixes or roots you recognize? What do they mean?	**pre** -- means before **exist** -- means something is there
2	What suffix endings does the word have? What do they mean? What is the word form - noun, verb, adjective, adverb, connector?	-ing don't know - could be verb, adjective, or noun
3	Look around the unknown word. What comes before it and what comes after? What's in the rest of the sentence?	**Before:** *individual's* - a noun -- 's shows possession, belongs to the individual **After:** *network* is a noun - so maybe preexisting is an adjective that tells what kind of networks there are
4	Guess about the meaning of the word. Good guess!	something that was there before - networks that were there before - that belong to an individual

Practice 13 Reading Word Attack Practice.

➜ **Task:** Work in small groups to attack the bolded words in the following sentences.

1. His chosen field was **physiology.**

Step	Question: PHYSIOLOGY	Answer
1	Are there any prefixes or roots you recognize? What do they mean?	
2	What suffix endings does the word have? What do they mean? What is the word form - noun, verb, adjective, adverb, connector?	
3	Look around the unknown word. What comes before it and what comes after? What's in the rest of the sentence?	**Before:** **After:**
4	Guess about the meaning of the word. Good guess!	

2. Pavlov's life was **uneventful** until he discovered what we call classical conditioning.

Step	Question: UNEVENTFUL	Answer
1	Are there any prefixes or roots you recognize? What do they mean?	
2	What suffix endings does the word have? What do they mean? What is the word form - noun, verb, adjective, adverb, connector?	
3	Look around the unknown word. What comes before it and what comes after? What's in the rest of the sentence?	**Before:** **After:**
4	Guess about the meaning of the word. Good guess!	

3. I somehow **irrationally** associate windchimes with being sad.

Step	Question: IRRATIONALLY	Answer
1	Are there any prefixes or roots you recognize? What do they mean?	
2	What suffix endings does the word have? What do they mean? What is the word form - noun, verb, adjective, adverb, connector?	
3	Look around the unknown word. What comes before it and what comes after? What's in the rest of the sentence?	**Before:** **After:**
4	Guess about the meaning of the word. Good guess!	

Practice 14

➜ **Task:**   Work in small groups to redo the Reading Sentence Completion Exercise from the pretest. This is located on the next two pages. Use the word attack skills you practiced above to ask yourself which word correctly fits in that sentence.

Reading Sentence Completion Exercise - PRETEST

Directions: In each box you will find four words to choose from. Underline or circle the word in each box that makes the sentence correct.

Example: Pavlov
<u>used</u>
using
useful
use
dogs in his research.

Pavlov, a Russian physiologist who
living
lived
live
lives
from 1849-1936,
was
knew
was knowing
was known
as quite a

successful
successfully
success
successes
medical scientist, but as a
theory
theoretical
theorist
theorize
he was not
near
nearly
nearness
nearer
as famous. His

theories
theory
theorist
theoretical
about the relationship between physiology and mental illness were not
wide
wider
widely
widest
accepted by

the other
researcher
researching
researches
researchers
of his day. They were just not
interesting
interested
interest
interests
in Pavlov's many
suggests
suggestion
suggestions
suggested

about mental illness. Despite his
dependence
depended
depend
dependably
on money from the government
does
did
is doing
to do
his

research and pay his
employers
employees
employment
employability
, Pavlov proved to be very out-spoken against the Communist party,

which he often
public
publicizes
publicly
publicity
denounced.   ➜ GO ON TO NEXT PAGE

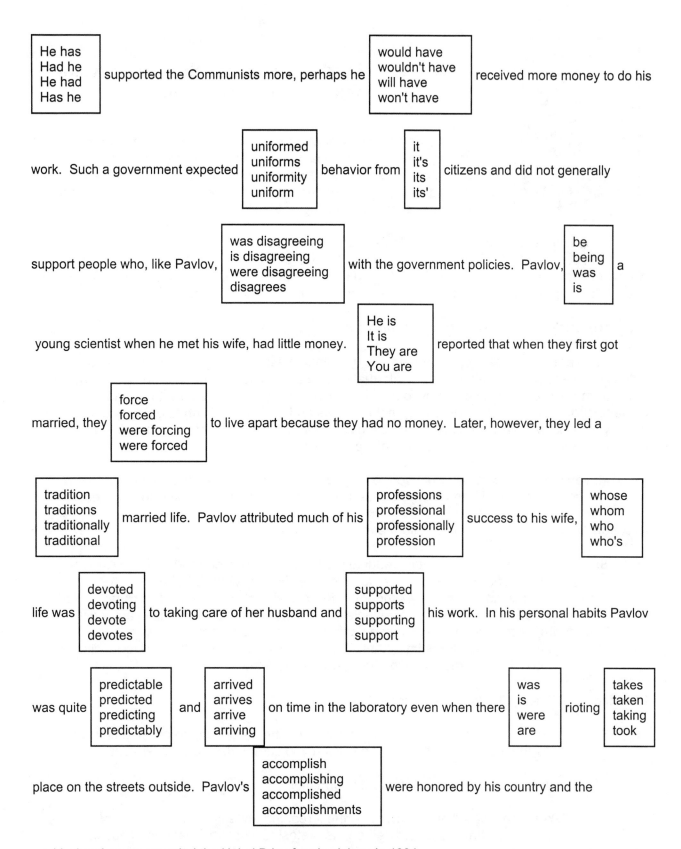

He has / Had he / He had / Has he supported the Communists more, perhaps he would have / wouldn't have / will have / won't have received more money to do his

work. Such a government expected uniformed / uniforms / uniformity / uniform behavior from it / it's / its / its' citizens and did not generally

support people who, like Pavlov, was disagreeing / is disagreeing / were disagreeing / disagrees with the government policies. Pavlov, be / being / was / is a

young scientist when he met his wife, had little money. He is / It is / They are / You are reported that when they first got

married, they force / forced / were forcing / were forced to live apart because they had no money. Later, however, they led a

tradition / traditions / traditionally / traditional married life. Pavlov attributed much of his professions / professional / professionally / profession success to his wife, whose / whom / who / who's

life was devoted / devoting / devote / devotes to taking care of her husband and supported / supports / supporting / support his work. In his personal habits Pavlov

was quite predictable / predicted / predicting / predictably and arrived / arrives / arrive / arriving on time in the laboratory even when there was / is / were / are rioting takes / taken / taking / took

place on the streets outside. Pavlov's accomplish / accomplishing / accomplished / accomplishments were honored by his country and the

world when he was awarded the Nobel Prize for physiology in 1904.

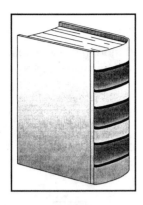

3. Reading Skills and Strategies; Note-taking and Summarizing

Knowing more vocabulary will help you become a better reader. In addition to learning more vocabulary, however, there are other ways you can become a better reader. In this part of the lesson, you will learn skills and strategies that good readers use for understanding textbook readings and for summarizing and taking notes from reading.

The lecture comprehension strategies you learned earlier in this lesson were divided into things you can do BEFORE, DURING, and AFTER the lecture. The reading skills and strategies can be divided the same way: 1) BEFORE you read, 2) DURING the reading, and 3) AFTER you read. We will practice these strategies in this lesson and the next lessons.

Why are underlining and good reading notes important?

The amount of reading you have to do in college classes is very heavy. You need to be able to read and pick out the important information by underlining in your textbook and/or by taking notes from the text. When you study for a test, you probably won't have time to reread everything in the textbook, so you will have to rely on your notes and your underlining to guide you to review the key information. *Selecting and understanding the important information is therefore the most important skill you need to have in academic textbook reading.*

If you underline carefully what you read, you will not have to read the whole text again. You can just read the important parts that you underlined. We will practice this skill in each lesson.

Practice 15   Finding the Important Information

➡ **TASK** :   You will find Dr. Tanner's reading on the next page. The reading is an excerpt from the textbook he uses, *Psychology for Teaching* by Guy R. Lefrançois (1991, Wadsworth Publishing Company). **Read the section entitled Learning.** Work in pairs, small groups, or as a whole class to decide which sentences are most important and underline those sentences. At the same time, cross out any sentences that are unimportant. Compare how you did on this exercise with how you did on the reading underlining during the test.

Practice 16   Finding the Important Information

➡ **TASK:**   Now underline the important information on the section in the reading entitled **Cognitivism**. This is the same section you summarized on the Pretest.

Next, cross out the unimportant information.

Your teacher will give you your Pretest reading underlining and summary back now. Compare what you underlined on the pretest to what you just underlined in this exercise. How are they different? Did you improve? Your teacher will show you what should have been underlined in this section and what parts should have been crossed out.

Reading Underlining PRETEST

Directions: Underline the important information as you read the entire page.

LEARNING

Conditioning is one form of learning. Learning is the acquisition of information and knowledge, of skills and habits, and of attitudes and beliefs. It always involves a change in one of these areas--a change that is brought about by the learner's experiences. Accordingly, psychologists define learning as all changes in behavior that result from experience, providing these changes are relatively permanent, do not result simply from growth or maturation, and are not the temporary effects of factors such as fatigue or drugs. Drug abuse was a big problem especially in the 1960s.

Change is interesting. Not all changes involved in learning are obvious and observable. For example, learning often involves changes in the learner's disposition--that is, in the person's inclination to do or not to do something. Hence changes in disposition have to do with motivation. Such changes cannot always be observed by teachers and others but are no less real or important.

Learning involves not only changes in disposition, but also changes in capability--that is, changes in the skills or knowledge required to do something (Gagne, 1985). Like changes in disposition, changes in capability cannot always be observed directly. To determine whether or not students' dispositions or capabilities have changed following instruction, teachers must provide them with an opportunity to engage in the relevant behavior. In most countries, teachers do not earn very much money. If instruction affects learners in such a way that their behaviors after instruction are observably different from those before instruction, we can conclude that learning has occurred. Even adults continue to learn all their lives.

BEHAVIORISM AND COGNITIVISM

Two major groups of theories relate to learning: behaviorism and cognitivism. Later you will read about several minor theories. Differences between these two major groups of learning theories center mainly on the questions each tries to answer. Behaviorism tries to explain simple behaviors--observable and predictable responses. Accordingly, it is concerned mainly with conditions (called stimuli) that affect organisms and that may lead to behavior, as well as with simple behaviors themselves (responses).

Behavior-oriented (or behavioristic) researchers attempt to discover the rules that govern the formation of relationships between stimuli and responses (the rules of conditioning). For this reason, behavioristic theories are often referred to as stimulus-response (S-R) theories. Researchers often use just one letter or symbol (such as S-R) to represent a word or concept.

In contrast to behaviorism, cognitive approaches deal primarily with questions relating to cognition, or knowing. Cognitive theorists are concerned with how we develop a fund of knowledge. Knowledge is power. Cognition-oriented researchers attempt to understand the nature of information--how it is acquired and organized by learners; how it can be recalled, modified, applied, and analyzed; and how the learner understands, evaluates, and controls the activities involved in cognition (metacognition).

COGNITIVISM

In a behavioristic analysis of learning, the primary emphasis is on the external conditions that affect behavior. In contrast to behaviorism, cognitivism involves the scientific study of mental events (E. Gagne, 1985, p. 4). Gagne was a professor at University of Iowa in the 1970s. Mental events have to do with acquiring, processing, storing, and retrieving information. Computers also process, store, and retrieve information. The primary emphasis in a cognitive analysis of learning is on the learner's mental structure, a concept that includes not only the learner's previous related knowledge, but also the strategies that the learner might bring to bear on the present situation. In this view, the explicit assumption is that learners are far from equal. It is the individual's preexisting network of concepts, strategies, and understanding that makes experience meaningful. Although learners may not be equal in the classroom, they are considered equal in a democracy.

Cognitivism focuses on knowledge; hence cognition is knowing. Cognition is a word used often in psychology books. One of the major emphases of cognitive approaches concerns the ways information is processed and stored. This departs dramatically from the major emphasis of a behavioristic approach, which involves behavior and its consequences.

What do good readers do before they begin reading?

Good readers look over the reading materials **before** they start reading. They look at the title, sub-titles or sub-headings, pictures and graphs, and the end of the reading. They make sure they have an idea of what the content of the reading is about before they start to read. This sets the stage in their mind for the reading; it gives them the "big picture" of what they are reading. Sometimes good readers start at the end of the reading if there is a summary of the content and read that first to get an idea of the content. If the text starts with a small summary (called an **abstract**), they start with that. Try this next time you have something to read! In the next lessons you will learn what good readers do during reading and after reading. You should also try to get the "big picture" before you take notes on reading and before you try to summarize the reading.

Why is summarizing so important?

When you write term papers or essays, you need to select information from several sources and put it together in your own words. This kind of *summary* writing or *summarizing* is an important skill you need for success in college classes. Rewriting or restating the information in your own words is important for two reasons. First, you can be sure that you understand the information completely if you are able to restate it in your own words.

Second, if you just copy verbatim (word for word) the phrases and sentences written by someone else and don't summarize it and integrate it with other information, you need to use quotation marks to show that these are someone else's words and ideas, and not yours.

If you do not use quotation marks, you are **plagiarizing**. **Plagiarism** means copying someone else's words but failing to let the reader know that these are not your words. All colleges and universities have strict rules about plagiarism because it is like stealing. A student who plagiarizes can receive an F or failing grade on the work in the course, or can even be expelled from the school. Plagiarism is a serious problem. For these reasons, to help understand the information and to avoid plagiarism, you need to be able to summarize important information in your own words.

You can put something into your own words by *paraphrasing*. Here's an example of *paraphrasing* of a sentence from the reading section.

"Cognitive theorists <u>are concerned with</u> how we <u>develop a fund of</u> knowledge."

<u>In my own words:</u> *Cognitive theorists <u>focus on</u> how we <u>continue to get more</u> knowledge.*
  (Note: Academic terms like *cognitive theorists* and *knowledge* don't need to be changed if you can't find the right words to express them.)

How to Summarize

There are several steps you can take to write a summary. We are going to practice these steps with the section on Cognitivism from the pretest. After you do these steps, you will look at the summary you wrote for the pretest and compare it to this model summary. Do this exercise with the whole class or in small groups.

1. First do the prereading task of looking for the "big picture" of the passage. Ask yourself, what is this about? What is the author trying to say here?

1. Answer: The paragraph is about cognitivism. I know that from the title. But the author

also writes about behaviorism and he compares these two approaches. So my summary should have information about both cognitivism and behaviorism, and should compare them.

2.   Find the most important information. Some of the information in the paragraph may not be important. We already practiced this task in the underlining exercise. When you summarize some information, you will probably include more details and more information than you did when you underlined.

2.   Answer: These are the most important sentence parts from the paragraph.

A. Behaviorism emphasizes the external conditions that affect behavior.
B. In contrast to behaviorism, cognitivism involves the scientific study of mental events.
C. Mental events are acquiring, processing, storing, and retrieving information.
D. The primary emphasis in a cognitive analysis of learning is on the learner's mental structure.
E. Mental structure includes previous related knowledge and strategies that the learner brings to the present situation.
F. The assumption is that learners are far from equal - they don't have the same mental structure.
G. The individual's preexisting network of concepts, strategies, and understanding makes experience meaningful.

3.   Read over the most important sentences to see how they are related to each other. Can you combine any of them? Is there information that is repeated? Is one sentence a definition that is related to another sentence? You are asking what each sentence does in the paragraph.

3.   Answer:

A.   is a definition or explanation of behaviorism.
B.   shows how cognitivism and behaviorism are different.
C.   is a definition of mental events.
D.   tells what the most important part of cognitive theory is.
E.   defines mental structure.
F.   says that learners are not equal.
G.   says that a person's network of ideas and strategies make experience meaningful.

4.   Decide how to organize your summary. What is the main topic of the paragraph? What is the main purpose? That should be stated in your first sentence. This is called a topic sentence.

4.   Answer.

Behaviorists and cognitivists look at learning in different ways.

Notice that this is not copied from the information -- it is not plagiarized. This is your own sentence that organizes the information you are summarizing. Now you are going to explain both theories and define the important concepts.

5. Decide the logical order in the rest of your paragraph. A logical order might be first to explain behaviorism and then to explain cognitivism. Then restate or paraphrase the important sentence parts that you identified in this order.

5. Answer. Here's how to organize the information and how it can be restated. In this example we decided to use the words cognitivists and behaviorists, the actual people who study these

theories, as the subjects of the sentences instead of using the fields of study, cognitivism and behaviorism. It is easier to form a sentence using a person as the subject rather than a field of study or idea as the subject. The table below shows what each sentence part does and how it can be paraphrased and summarized.

Sentence Part	What it is	Combining or paraphrasing in my words
The main idea – the big picture	contrast and explanation of behaviorism and cognitivism	Behaviorists and cognitivists look at learning in different ways.
A. Behaviorism emphasizes the external conditions that affect behavior	a definition or explanation of behaviorism	Behaviorists look at the external things that change behavior.
B. In contrast to behaviorism, cognitivism involves the scientific study of mental events	shows how cognitivism and behaviorism are different	In contrast, cognitivists study mental events.
C. Mental events are acquiring, processing, storing, and retrieving information.	a definition of mental events	Mental events are the ways we get, use, store, and remember information.
D. The primary emphasis in a cognitive analysis of learning is on the learner's mental structure.	tells what the most important part of the cognitive theory is	Cognitivists think that the student's mental structure is very important.
E. Mental structure includes previous related knowledge and strategies that the learner brings to the present situation.	defines mental structure	Mental structure means what people already know and what strategies they have for learning.
F. The assumption is that learners are far from equal -- they don't have the same mental structure.	says that cognitivists assume learners are not equal	Cognitivists believe that students don't all start out with the same (equal) mental structures.

G. The individual's preexisting network of concepts, strategies, and understanding makes experience meaningful.	says that a person's different network of ideas and strategies make experience meaningful	[*In a summary, this information turns out to be not so important so we decide not to include it. It just states again the idea that people are not equal - they have different preexisting mental structures.*]

Practice 17

➜ **Task**: Compare your summary from the Pretest to this model summary below. Work with a partner and help each other answer the following questions.

☞ Did my summary include the important information? If not, what did I leave out?

☞ Did my summary include any of the unimportant information? If so, what is it and what should I leave out?

☞ Is there any plagiarism? Did I copy sentences verbatim? If so, try rewriting the sentences that are verbatim.

Model Answer for Pretest Summary:

Behaviorists and cognitivists look at learning in different ways. Behaviorists look at the external things that change behavior. In contrast, cognitivists study mental events. Mental events are the ways we get, use, store, and remember information. Cognitivists think that the student's mental structure is very important. Mental structure means what people already know and what strategies they have for learning. Cognitivists believe that students don't all start out with the same (equal) mental structures.

Reading Note-taking

COGNITIVISM

In a behavioristic analysis of learning, the primary emphasis is on the external conditions that affect behavior. In contrast to behaviorism, cognitivism involves the scientific study of mental events (E. Gagne, 1985, p. 4). Gagne was a professor at University of Iowa in the 1970s. Mental events have to do with acquiring, processing, storing, and retrieving information. Computers also process, store, and retrieve information. The primary emphasis in a cognitive analysis of learning is on the learner's mental structure, a concept that includes not only the learner's previous related knowledge, but also the strategies that the learner might bring to bear on the present situation. In this view, the explicit assumption is that learners are far from equal. It is the individual's preexisting network of concepts, strategies, and understanding that makes experience meaningful. Although learners may not be equal in the classroom, they are considered equal in a democracy.

Practice 18 Reading Notes Practice. Most college students take notes from the textbooks and other materials they read. Often they put these notes on the opposite page of their lecture notes so they can study their lecture notes, complete missing parts of their lecture notes, or add information from the textbook to the lecture information.

➜ **TASK**: Practice your note-taking skills with the part of the reading in the shaded box, which is repeated above this exercise. You can do this by yourself or with a partner. When you take notes from a textbook, you should use the same system of symbols and abbreviations you used in your lecture notes. Do not look at the model notes on the next page while you do this exercise!

_____

_____

_____

_____

_____

_____

_____

_____

_____

_____

_____

_____

_____

Model Reading Notes

Cog-ism = sci. study of mental events → = acquire,
                                            process,
    ↓   store, &
≠ B-ism - emphasizes conditions   retrieve info.
            that affect behav.
cog - learner's mental structure =
                        1) prev. knowledge
    ↓   2) learning strategies
assumes learners ≠ because preexisting networks =
                        1 - concepts
                        2 - strategies
                        3 -understanding

4. Sentence Complexity

* Albert Einstein (1879-1955). Einstein was born in Germany. He was a physicist and famous for his Theory of Relativity. In 1921 he won the Nobel Prize for Physics.

Academic writing and speech often use long, complex sentences. Through analysis of many college textbooks and lectures, a determination was made of which kinds of complex sentences are used the most in academic language. This lesson and the following lessons will help you to learn to understand these complex sentences. By practicing, you can learn to "pull apart" these sentences and understand their parts. This practice will help make reading academic language easier.

Conditional Sentences: If ... then

➜ **Task**:   Read this information as a whole class.

This type of sentence is called conditional because two things are happening in the sentence, and they depend on each other in some way.

For example, Dr. Tanner said:

If I deny you food, **then** you get hungry.

Often the word then is left out of the sentence, but it means the same thing.

If I deny you food, you get hungry.

This kind of sentence is made of two shorter sentences that are connected or related to each other with the **if ... then** connector.

A. I deny you food.
B. You get hungry.

Another example from Dr. Tanner's lecture is:

If I blow in your eye, you blink.

A. I blow in your eye.
B. You blink

A ➜ B   One-way conditional

In the two example sentences above, the relationship between sentence A and sentence B is only in one direction. We call this a one-way conditional sentence. In other words, A causes B, but B does not cause A.

40

You CAN'T say, for example:

> If you get hungry, I deny you food   NO!

> If you blink, I blow in your eye.   NO!

A ⟷ B   Two-way conditional.

In another kind of conditional sentence, A and B can be reversed and the sentence still makes sense.

For example, the A and B parts of this sentence can be reversed and the they still make sense.

> If you learned something, then your behavior changed.

> If your behavior changed, then you learned something.

Practice 19

➜ **Task:**   Whole-class or small group activity. Use familiar people and events (class members, sports events, news stories) to make both kinds of conditional sentences.

Discuss each sentence as being one-way or two-way:

One-way: A ➜ B

_____

Two-way: A ⟷ B

_____

Practice 20

➜ **Task:**   As a whole class, read the following sentence from the textbook and discuss its meaning. Which part is A and which is B? Is there a one-way or two-way relationship between A and B?

If instruction affects learners in such a way that their behaviors after instruction are observably different from those before instruction, then we can conclude that learning has occurred.

5. Academic Culture

A New Culture

When you start college, you are entering a new world or a new culture. The language is different from the language you speak at home and with friends. These lessons are designed not only to help you develop academic language skills, but also to understand the academic culture. Each lesson, including this lesson related to the pretest, has information about professors and the academic culture.

The Professor

The teachers or instructors in a four-year college or university usually have a doctoral degree or doctorate. Dr. David Tanner, the professor in the pretest lecture, has a doctorate in educational psychology. The letters he uses after his name are Ph.D., which stands for Doctor of Philosophy, the name of the degree most professors in almost every area of study have. Some professors of education have Ed.D. after their name, which indicates Doctor of Education. People with either degree should be addressed as 'doctor'.

Teachers whose job title is lecturer or instructor often do not have the doctoral degree. People with professor as their job title usually have the doctorate degree. Within the title of professor there are three levels: assistant professor, associate professor, and full professor. Faculty usually start out as assistant professors after they receive their doctoral degree and then are promoted up to associate and full professor after several years of teaching, doing research, publishing scholarly papers, and doing other academic work.

In order to stay at an institution, a professor must be awarded tenure before seven years pass. If the professor does not get tenure, he or she must leave the institution and look for another job. Tenure requires that the professor be a good teacher, do important service to the community and the school, and publish in his or her field. Publication includes books, book chapters in an edited book, and research journal articles in scientific research journals. Faculty have described this tenure and promotion system as the "publish or perish" system for many years. Some institutions also expect that faculty will compete for and get money to support projects and research, called grant money. Faculty write a proposal for a project or research and request money to support this work. Grant money usually comes from the national government, the state government, or private foundations that give money for research.

ALADIN Dictionary Lesson 1

Table of Contents

1. Thinking — Page 45

2. Person Characteristics — Page 47

3. Importance — Page 49

4. Information — Page 50

5. Research, Academic — Page 50

6. Cause-effect, Change — Page 52

7. Hedge, Qualify — Page 53

8. History, Government, Society — Page 54

9. Time — Page 54

10. Connectors and Comparisons — Page 55

11. Evaluation and Description — Page 56

Alphabetical list of Words/Phrases and Page Numbers in Lesson 1 Dictionary

accordingly	55
acquisition	52
apparatus	50
approach ✔	50
as follows	55
associate with	55
assumption	45
attentive	45, 47
attribute to	52
bare my soul ✔	45
behaviorist ✄	51
being ✔	47
bring to bear ✔	52
capability	47
capacity ✔	47
claim to fame	49
classical	49, 54
code	50
cognitivist ✄	45, 51
comparatively youthful ✔	53, 54
concept	45
conclude	45, 56
consequence	52
consistently	47, 54
context	50
deal with	50
demonstrate	51
deny ✔	52
departs dramatically from	55
discipline ✔	51
discomfort ✄	47
disposition	48
either ... or	55
element	56
emphasize	49
empirically	51
engage in ✔	45
essential	49
evaluate	45, 56
event	54
explicit	50

Word/Phrase	Page
external	56
extinguish	52
extract ✄	45, 52
fairly youthful ✔	53
fatigue	48
field ✔	51
figure out	45
focus on	45
formation	52
frequently	54
fund of knowledge ✔	50
fundamental	49
hence	55
illogical ✄	46
illogically ✄	48
in fact	55
in contrast to	55
in terms of	55
inclination ✄	48
indeed	55
influence	52
inner-city	54
irrationally ✄	46, 48
lecture	51
likely	53
mainly	53
major	49
make sense	46
maturation	48, 52
melancholy	48
mental	46
mental structure	51
metacogni-tion ✄	46
modify	52
motivation	48, 53
network ✄	50
not only ... but also	56
notion	46
observable	56
organism	51
perception	46
physiology	51
pointless ✄✔	46
predict ✄	44, 54

Word/Phrase	Page
predictable ✄	56
preexisting ✄	55
presume ✄	46
previous	55
primarily	49, 53
profoundly	46, 49
rational	46, 48
recall ✔	46
recognize✄✔	46
related knowledge	56
relevant	49
research-oriented	51
response	53
restrict	47, 53
retrieve	47
rules that govern ✔	54
salivation	48
secretion	48
so to speak ✔	53
speculate	47
stimulus	53
strategy	47
symbol	50
that is	56
the nature of	56
theorist	51
theory	47
ultimately	55
universal ✄	49
validate	51
visceral	48
whether...or not	56

1. Thinking

Noun	Verb	Adjective	Adverb	Brief Definition	Example
assumption	assume			n. an idea believed to be true	The **assumption** is that there is a set of universal laws.
attention	attend to, pay attention to	**attentive**	attentively	adj. looking at carefully, paying a lot of attention to	The animals began to salivate and they were very, very **attentive** to this.
	bare my soul ✔			v. tell your secret thoughts	I will **bare my soul** to you.
cognitivist ✂ cognition cognitivism		cognitive	cognitively	n. scientist who studies the mental process of knowing or learning	**Cognitivists** are interested in how we develop knowledge.
concept conception	conceive conceptualize	conceptual	conceptually	n. an idea about something	Learners have a network of **concepts** and strategies that help them learn.
conclusion	**conclude**	conclusive	conclusively	v. decide something after seeing the facts	If behaviors change, we can **conclude** that learning has occurred.
engagement in	**engage in** ✔	engaged in		v. do something, participate in	Teachers must provide them with an opportunity to **engage in** the important behavior.
evaluation	**evaluate**	evaluative		v. think about or study something and decide whether it is good or bad	Learners **evaluate** all new information.
extraction	**extract** ✂	extractable		v. get, get from, get out of	I could watch a dog and **extract** from that animal's behavior some kind of code that helps me explain its behavior.
	figure out			v. understand, explain	We **figure out** how these changes in behavior occur.
focus	**focus on**	focused		v. concentrate on or think about one thing	Behaviorists **focused on** observable learning.

Noun	Verb	Adjective	Adverb	Brief Definition	Example
illogic		**illogical** ✂	illogically	adj. without logic, irrational.	My dislike of wind chimes is **illogical**.
		irrational	**irrationally** ✂	adv. without logical, clear thinking	I somehow **irrationally** associate wind chimes with sadness.
	make sense			v. think or speak rationally, understandably	It doesn't **make any sense** not to like science.
mentality		**mental**	mentally	adj. having to do with thinking, the brain - not physical	Cognitivists analyze the learners' **mental** structures.
metacognition ✂		metacognitive	metacogni-tively	n. meta=beyond; beyond or above cognition	The learner understands and controls the activities involved in cognition (**metacognition**).
notion				n. an idea, opinion or belief about something	That universality **notion** is very important.
perception	perceive	perceptive perceivable	perceptively	n. belief or opinion you have after you observe something	Some psychologists have a negative **perception** of behaviorists and their research.
pointlessness		**pointless** ✂ ✔	pointlessly	adj. without any meaning or reason	It's **pointless** to say that's not rational.
prediction	**predict** ✂	predictive predictable	predictably	v. believe something will happen in the future	Behaviorists try to **predict** what the animal will do.
presumption	**presume** ✂	presumptive	presumably	v. believe something to be true	Let's **presume** you are the science teacher.
profundity		profound	**profoundly**	adv. very, greatly, or strongly	Pavlov's explanation of learning is a **profoundly** important one.
rationality	rationalize	**rational**	rationally	adj. logical, based on clear thinking	Disliking wind chimes is not **rational.**
recall	**recall** ✔	recalled		v. remember	They attempt to understand how information can be **recalled**.
recognition	**recognize** ✂ ✔	recognized recognizable	recognizably	v. understand, accept that something is correct	Pavlov **recognized** that salivation occurs even if the dogs get no food.

46

Noun	Verb	Adjective	Adverb	Brief Definition	Example
restriction	**restrict**	restrictive restricted	restrictively	v. limit, keep narrow, keep small	They **restrict** their explanation of learning to things they can directly observe.
retrieval	**retrieve**	retrievable		v. get back again	Mental events have to do with **retrieving** information.
speculator speculation	**speculate**	speculative	speculatively	v. to guess, wonder about something	They didn't **speculate** about mental processes.
strategy	strategize	strategic	strategically	n. a plan for doing something	One **strategy** for learning new vocabulary is to use a new word several times a week.
theory theorist	theorize	theoretical	theoretically	n. a scientific idea or explanation	Pavlov developed a **theory** about how animals and people learn.

2. Person Characteristics

Noun	Verb	Adjective	Adverb	Definition	Example
attention	attend to; (also, pay attention to)	**attentive**	attentively	adj. think about, look at, pay lots of attention to	They were very very **attentive** to the dogs' salivation.
being ✔				n. existence, living, being a live person	It isn't a learned response, it is part of your **being**.
capability		capable	capably	n. can do something, has the ability	Learning also involves changes in **capability**.
capacity ✔				n. ability to do something	He won a Nobel Prize for his **capacity** to measure salivary secretions in dogs.
consistency		consistent	**consistently**	adv. repeatedly, the same thing over and over	They ring a bell before they present food and they do that **consistently**.
discomfort ✂	discomfort	discomforting		n. feeling bad, uncomfortable	Children come to associate the **discomfort** of hunger with science.

Noun	Verb	Adjective	Adverb	Definition	Example
disposition				n. attitude toward something	Learning involves changes in the learner's **disposition** - that is, in the person's inclination to do or not do something.
fatigue	fatigue	fatigued		n. feeling very tired	Learning is change that can't be attributed to **fatigue**.
illogic		illogical	**illogically** ✂	adv. not logical, not correct thinking	I somehow **illogically**, irrationally associate the presence of windchimes with being sad.
inclination ✂	incline	inclined		n. willingness to do something	The learner's **inclination** to do something changes.
irrationality		irrational	**irrationally** ✂	adv. not logical, not rational	I somehow illogically, **irrationally** associate the presence of windchimes with being sad.
maturation maturity	mature	mature	maturely	n. growing up, getting older	Learning is change not attributed to **maturation**.
melancholy		melancholy melancholic		n. sadness	When I hear windchimes I feel a sense of sadness or **melancholy**.
motivation motive	motivate	motivated		n. want to do something, have reason to do something	Hence changes in disposition have to do with **motivation**.
rationality	rationalize	**rational**	rationally	adj. logical, makes sense	That's not a **rational** relationship.
salivation saliva	salivate	salivary		n. making the water in your mouth	He measured **salivation** in dogs.
secretion	secrete	secretory		n. the release of water or liquid	The dog has an automatic response and **secretion** begins.
viscera		**visceral**	viscerally	adj. gut reaction, automatic reaction	It is automatic - a **visceral** response.

3. Importance

Noun	Verb	Adjective	Adverb	Definition	Example
claim to fame				n. the thing that makes you famous	How would you like measuring dog salivation to be your **claim to fame**?
classic		**classical**	classically	adj. first, original, standard, most important	His theory is so fundamental to the field that it is called **classical** conditioning.
emphasis	**emphasize**	emphatic	emphatically	v. put the most attention on	Behaviorists **emphasize** observable learning.
essentialness essence		**essential**	essentially	adj. very important, fundamental	The **essential** elements of the situation are as follows.
fundamental		**fundamental**	fundamentally	adj. very important, essential	His theory is so **fundamental** to learning theory.
majority		**major**		adj. big, important, most	There are differences between these two **major** learning theories.
primacy		primary	**primarily**	adv. first, mostly, most importantly	Cognitive approaches deal **primarily** with questions related to knowing.
profundity		profound	**profoundly**	adv. very, greatly or strongly	Pavlov's explanation of learning is a **profoundly** important one.
relevance		**relevant**	relevantly	adj. important, related in an important way	Teachers provide students with opportunities to engage in **relevant** behaviors.
universality universe		**universal** ✂	universally	adj. found everywhere, for everyone	There is a set of **universal** laws of learning.

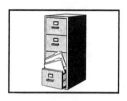

4. Information

Noun	Verb	Adjective	Adverb	Definition	Example
code codification	code codify	coded codified		n. system of rules or system of information	We extract a **code** from the animal's behavior to help explain the changes in behavior.
context	contextualize	contextual	contextually	n. background information, setting	I will provide a little bit of **context** for this lecture.
	deal with			v. use, work with, are about	Cognitive approaches **deal with** knowing.
explicitness		**explicit**	explicitly	adj. said directly and clearly, not implied	The **explicit** assumption is that learners are not equal.
fund of knowledge ✔				n. amount of our knowledge, what we know	Cognitivists study how we develop a **fund of knowledge**.
network ✂	network	networked		n. arrangement of information, all connected	Learners have a preexisting **network** of concepts.
symbol symbolism	symbolize	symbolic	symbolically	n. something that represents another thing or idea	Researchers use a letter or **symbol** to represent a word or concept.

5. Research, Academic

Noun	Verb	Adjective	Adverb	Definition	Example
apparatus				n. equipment, machine	I have seen drawings of the **apparatus** Pavlov used.
approach ✔	approach	approachable		n. the way you start to do some work or research	Cognitive **approaches** to learning theory deal with knowing.

Noun	Verb	Adjective	Adverb	Definition	Example
behavior behaviorism **behaviorist** ✂	behave	behavioral	behaviorally	n. person in psychology who studies how people react or behave	And these **behaviorists** focus on observable learning.
cognition cognitivism **cognitivist** ✂		cognitive	cognitively	n. a person in psychology who studies how people think	**Cognitivists** study mental events.
demonstration	**demonstrate**	demonstra- ted		v. to show something	He **demonstrated** that he could measure how much the animal salivated.
discipline ✔		disciplinary		n. type of academic work	That **discipline** is comparatively youthful.
empiricism empiricist		empirical	**empirically**	adv. proved scientifically or observed	There is no way to **empirically** validate that kind of assumption.
field ✔				n. type or area of work or study	Educational psychology is a fairly youthful **field**.
lecture lecturer	lecture			n. talk by a professor in a college class	Today's **lecture** is on an element of learning theory.
mental structure				n. the way thinking is organized in the brain	Cognitivists analyze the learners' **mental structures**.
organism				n. something that's alive	Stimuli are conditions that affect **organisms**.
physiology		physiological	physiologically	n. the study of how living things exist and grow	His chosen field was **physiology**.
		research- oriented		adj. work that is related to scientific research	The careful, **research-oriented** work began a hundred years ago.
theory **theorist**	theorize	theoretical	theoretically	n. person or scientist who creates ideas about how something happens	One branch of learning theory is made up of **theorists** who are called behaviorists.
validity validation	**validate**	valid	validly	v. show something to be true, correct, or accurate	There is no way to empirically **validate** that kind of assumption.

6. Cause-Effect, Change

Noun	Verb	Adjective	Adverb	Definition	Example
acquisition	acquire	acquired		n. getting something	Learning is the **acquisition** of information and knowledge.
attribution	**attribute to**	attributed		v. say who or what caused something	Learning is change that can't be **attributed to** age.
	bring to bear ✔			v. bring influence on, use	They study strategies that learners **bring to bear** on the situation.
consequence		consequential	consequentially	n. result, what happened	The behavioristic approach emphasized behavior and its **consequences**.
denial	**deny** ✔	deniable	deniably	v. keep something away from you	If I deny you food, then you get hungry.
extinction	**extinguish**	extinct		v. stop something	The animal stops salivating and this behavior is **extinguished**.
extraction	**extract** ✂	extractable		v. get out of, take out, get from, get	They **extract** a code from the animal's behavior.
formation	form	formed formative		n. something made or created	They study the **formation** of relationships between stimuli and responses.
influence	influence	influential	influentially	n. part of cause, reason something happens	Learning is change that can't be attributed to some chemical **influence**.
maturation maturity	mature	mature	maturely	n. growing up, getting older	Learning is change not attributed to **maturation**.
modification	**modify**	modified modifiable		v. change something	They study how information is acquired and **modified**.

52

Noun	Verb	Adjective	Adverb	Definition	Example
motivation motive	motivate	motivated		n. want to do something, have reason to do something	Hence changes in disposition have to do with **motivation**.
response	respond	responsive	responsively	n. an action taken as a result of something	Connected with this stimulus we have a **response**.
restriction	**restrict**	restrictive	restrictively	v. keep under control, not free, limited	They **restrict** their explanation of learning to things they can observe.
stimulus stimulant	stimulate	stimulated		n. something that causes a response	In this kind of learning we have an unconditioned **stimulus**.

7. Hedge, Qualify

Hedge Word or Phrase, Qualifier	Explanation	Example
comparatively youthful ✔	not really young, but somewhat young compared to other fields and other sciences	Educational psychology is a **comparatively youthful** discipline.
fairly youthful ✔	relatively young, not old, not young; not as old as many fields	It is a **fairly youthful** field.
likely	probably, in all likelihood	You have **likely** heard his name (Pavlov).
mainly	mostly, not all, more than half	Behaviorism is concerned **mainly** with stimuli that affect organisms.
primarily	firstly, mostly, mainly, not all	Cognitive approaches deal **primarily** with knowing.
so to speak ✔	this is one way to say it, it can be said this way	This guy is coming down the hall **so to speak** and the animals begin to salivate.

8. History, Government, Society

Noun	Verb	Adjective	Adverb	Definition	Example
		inner-city		adj. people in the center of the city, usually poor	Let's say you teach in an **inner-city** school where some of the children are poor.
rules that govern ✔				n. guidelines, laws that control	Researchers attempt to discover the **rules that govern** the relationships between stimuli and responses.

9. Time

Noun	Verb	Adjective	Adverb	Definition	Example
		comparatively youthful ✔		not old, not young recent in time compared to other fields	Educational psychology is a **comparatively youthful** discipline.
classic		**classical**	classically	adj. first, original, standard, most important	His theory is so fundamental to the field that it is called **classical** conditioning.
consistency		consistent	**consistently**	adv. repeatedly, over and over the same	We ring a bell before they present food and they do that **consistently**.
event		eventful		n. something that happens at a particular time	Cognitivism involves the scientific study of mental **events**.
frequency	frequent	frequent	**frequently**	adv. often, quite often	**Frequently** classical conditioning is called accidental learning.
prediction	**predict** ✂	predictive predictable	predictably	v. believe something will happen in the future	Behaviorists try to **predict** what the animal will do.

Noun	Verb	Adjective	Adverb	Definition	Example
	preexist	**preexisting** ✂		adj. was there before	The individual's **preexisting** network of concepts makes experience meaningful.
		previous	previously	adj. something that happened before	Mental structure includes the learner's **previous** related knowledge.
ultimate		ultimate	**ultimately**	adv. in the end, it happens at last	**Ultimately** the animal stops salivating.

10. Connectors and Comparisons

Connector	Meaning and Use	Example
accordingly	for that reason, therefore, as a result	Behaviorism tries to explain observable responses. **Accordingly**, it is concerned with stimuli.
as follows	more information comes next	I'd like to provide you a little context for the lecture **as follows**.
associate with	A is related to B, A is linked to B	Something occurred that I **associate with** windchimes.
departs dramatically from (dramatically different)	A is very different from B, contrasting A and B	Cognitive approaches **depart dramatically from** behavioral approaches.
either ... or	either A or B, only one, not both A and B	**Either** they get up so late in the morning that they don't have time for breakfast **or** there is no food and they don't eat.
hence	therefore; A is true, therefore B; as a result of A we have B	Cognitivism focuses on knowledge; **hence** cognition is knowing.
in contrast to	A is different from B	**In contrast to** behaviorism, cognitivism involves the study of mental events.
in fact	add more information to A	His chosen field was physiology, and **in fact**, he won a Nobel Prize for his work.
in terms of	specific information about A	**In terms of** the theory, here's what happens.
indeed	in fact, actually, as expected - more information, true information	They found **indeed** that this was the case.

Connector	Meaning and Use	Example
not only ... but also	not just A, but also includes B; both A and B	Mental structure includes **not only** previous knowledge **but also** strategies.
related knowledge	knowledge of A is related to knowledge of B, A is associated with B	Mental structure includes the learner's previous **related knowledge**.
that is	in other words; a restatement	Learning often involves changes in the learner's disposition – **that is**, in the person's inclination to do or not to do something.
whether ... or not	A doesn't matter, we will have B anyhow	The animal salivates **whether or not** we present food.

11. Evaluation, Description

Noun	Verb	Adjective	Adverb	Definition	Example
conclusion	**conclude**	conclusive	conclusively	v. decide something after seeing the facts	If behaviors change, we can **conclude** that learning has occurred.
element		elemental		n. a part	Today's lecture is on an **element** of learning theory.
evaluation	**evaluate**	evaluative		v. think about or study something and decide whether it is good or bad	Learners **evaluate** all new information.
	externalize	**external**	externally	adj. outside, not internal or inside	The primary emphasis is on **external** conditions that affect behavior.
observation	observe	**observable**	observably	adj. can be seen	Behaviorists are interested in **observable** changes in behavior.
prediction	predict	**predictable** ✂	predictably	adj. easy to guess in advance about something	Behaviorism tries to explain observable and **predictable** behaviors.
the nature of				n. the way something is, how it is	Researchers attempt to understand **the nature of** information.

Academic **L**anguage: **A**ssessment and **D**evelopment of **I**ndividual **N**eeds

LADIN

Lesson 2

ALADIN Lesson 2 Table of Contents

Table of Contents 58

Self Assessments of Lesson Vocabulary 59

1. Note-taking - Lecture has three segments of about 10 minutes 61

    A. Lecture Note-taking 61

        Lecture Part A Note-taking (no prior reading) 62
        Lecture Question Part A 63
        Reading for Lecture Part B: Excerpts from 64
            The House on Mango Street 64
                "The House on Mango Street" 64
                "A House of My Own" 65
                "My Name" 65
        Lecture Part B Note-taking 66
        Lecture Question Part B 67
        Reading for Lecture Part C: Excerpts from 68
            The House on Mango Street 68
                "Four Skinny Trees" 68
                "The Three Sisters" 68
                "Mango Says Goodbye Sometimes" 70
        Lecture Part C Note-taking 71
        Lecture Question Part C 72
        Lecture Signals and Note-taking Skills 73

    B. Reading Note-taking and Summaries 77
        Reading Part 1 78
        Reading Part 2 80

2. Academic Vocabulary Building 82
    Word Attack Skills and Review 82
    Roots, Prefixes, and Suffixes 83
    Noun Forms 87
    Verbs 89
    Word Attack 90
    Endings Exercise 91

3. Reading 92

4. Sentence Complexity : Conditional Review and Nominalization 98

5. Academic Culture 100

Dictionary Lesson 2 Dr. Reuben Sanchez 103

Lesson 2 VOCABULARY SELF-ASSESSMENT - READING

DIRECTIONS: Circle the number that shows how well you know each word below.	1 I don't recognize this word.	2 I've seen this word before but I don't know what it means.	3 I think I know what this word means but I am not 100% sure.	4 I know what this word means and I can probably use it in a sentence.	5 I know this word and I have used it recently in speaking or writing.
1. confusion	1	2	3	4	5
2. precise	1	2	3	4	5
3. despite	1	2	3	4	5
4. society	1	2	3	4	5
5. relevant	1	2	3	4	5
6. profound	1	2	3	4	5
7. baptize	1	2	3	4	5
8. dominated	1	2	3	4	5
9. reputation	1	2	3	4	5
10. symbolically	1	2	3	4	5
11. ambition	1	2	3	4	5
12. conception	1	2	3	4	5
13. sophisticated	1	2	3	4	5
14. inherited	1	2	3	4	5
15. presumably	1	2	3	4	5
16. literary	1	2	3	4	5
17. simplistic	1	2	3	4	5
18. colloquial	1	2	3	4	5
19. narrative	1	2	3	4	5
20. vignette	1	2	3	4	5
21. patriarchal	1	2	3	4	5
22. dissertation	1	2	3	4	5
23. protagonist	1	2	3	4	5
24. omniscient	1	2	3	4	5
25. genre	1	2	3	4	5

Lesson 2 VOCABULARY SELF-ASSESSMENT - DICTATION

DIRECTIONS: Write each word you hear. Then circle the number that shows how well you know each word you write below.	1 I don't recognize this word.	2 I've **seen** this word before but I don't know what it means.	3 I **think** I know what this word means but I am not 100% sure.	4 I know what this word means and I can **probably** use it in a sentence.	5 I know this word and I have used it recently in speaking or writing.
1.	1	2	3	4	5
2.	1	2	3	4	5
3.	1	2	3	4	5
4.	1	2	3	4	5
5.	1	2	3	4	5
6.	1	2	3	4	5
7.	1	2	3	4	5
8.	1	2	3	4	5
9.	1	2	3	4	5
10.	1	2	3	4	5
11.	1	2	3	4	5
12.	1	2	3	4	5
13.	1	2	3	4	5
14.	1	2	3	4	5
15.	1	2	3	4	5
16.	1	2	3	4	5
17.	1	2	3	4	5
18.	1	2	3	4	5
19.	1	2	3	4	5
20.	1	2	3	4	5
21.	1	2	3	4	5
22.	1	2	3	4	5
23.	1	2	3	4	5
24.	1	2	3	4	5
25.	1	2	3	4	5

Lesson 2   Dr. Reuben Sanchez
English Department

The House on Mango Street
by Sandra Cisneros.
1989. New York: Vintage Contemporaries.

1. Note-taking

This lesson begins with an academic vocabulary self-assessment. At the end of this lesson you may do this assessment again. Self-assessment is a very good way to find out what you know and how well you know it. There is no grade on this assessment. It is just used to help you and your instructor know what your starting knowledge level is on some of the academic vocabulary.

In Lesson 2 you will listen to a lecture by a professor, Dr. Reuben Sanchez, from the English Department. The lecture is divided into three ten-minute segments. You will be taking notes on each segment. Before Part B and Part C of the lecture, you will be reading short excerpts from the novel Dr. Sanchez is lecturing about, *The House on Mango Street* by Sandra Cisneros.

Each lecture section also has a question you will answer using your lecture notes. After you answer the questions, the instructor will show you model answers for your notes and for the questions.

In the second part of the lesson, you will be underlining and taking notes from some academic reading about the author, Sandra Cisneros, and about other related issues. You will also write a summary of the reading. Your instructor will show you model reading summaries and notes.

The rest of the lesson, like Lesson 1, includes reading strategies, academic vocabulary building, practice with long sentences, and academic culture.

LESSON 2 LECTURE NOTES   Part A

Use the following two pages to take notes from Part A of the lecture. This section is about 11 minutes long. The information in your notes will be used to answer a question later.

_____

_____
_____
_____
_____
_____
_____
_____
_____
_____
_____
_____
_____
_____
_____
_____
_____
_____
_____
_____
_____
_____
_____
_____
_____

Continue Taking Notes on Next Page

_____

_____

_____

_____

_____

_____

_____

_____

_____

_____

_____

_____

Lecture Question Part A

Use your lecture notes from **Part A** to answer the following question. Use complete sentences.

What is the term that Dr. Sanchez uses that refers to a novel of education or formation? Briefly explain what this term means and how it relates to the lecture topic.

_____

_____

_____

_____

_____

_____

_____

_____

_____

_____

Chapters (Vignettes) Dr. Sanchez refers to in Lecture Part B - Read before watching Lecture Part B

"The House on Mango Street"

We didn't always live on Mango Street. Before that we lived on Loomis on the third floor, and before that we lived on Keeler. Before Keeler it was Paulina, and before that I can't remember. But what I remember most is moving a lot. Each time it seemed there'd be one more of us. By the time we got to Mango Street we were six--Mama, Papa, Carlos, Kiki, my sister Nenny and me.

The house on Mango Street is ours, and we don't have to pay rent to anybody, or share the yard with the people downstairs, or be careful not to make too much noise, and there isn't a landlord banging on the ceiling with a broom. But even so, it's not the house we'd thought we'd get.

We had to leave the flat on Loomis quick. The water pipes broke and the landlord wouldn't fix them because the house was too old. We had to leave fast. We were using the washroom next door and carrying water over in empty milk gallons. That's why Mama and Papa looked for a house, and that's why we moved into the house on Mango Street, far away, on the other side of town.

They always told us that one day we would move into a house, a real house that would be ours for always so we wouldn't have to move each year. And our house would have running water and pipes that worked. And inside it would have real stairs, not hallway stairs, but stairs inside like the houses on T.V. And we'd have a basement and at least three washrooms so when we took a bath we wouldn't have to tell everybody. Our house would be white with trees around it, a great big yard and grass growing without a fence. This was the house Papa talked about when he held a lottery ticket and this was the house Mama dreamed up in the stories she told us before we went to bed.

But the house on Mango Street is not the way they told it at all. It's small and red with tight steps in front and windows so small you'd think they were holding their breath. Bricks are crumbling in places, and the front door is so swollen you have to push hard to get in. There is no front yard, only four little elms the city planted by the curb. Out back is a small garage for the car we don't own yet and a small yard that looks smaller between the two buildings on either side. There are stairs in our house, but they're ordinary hallway stairs, and the house has only one washroom. Everybody has to share a bedroom--Mama and Papa, Carlos and Kiki, me and Nenny.

Once when we were living on Loomis, a nun from my school passed by and saw me playing out front. The Laundromat downstairs had been boarded up because it had been robbed two days before and the owner had painted on the wood YES WE'RE OPEN so as not to lose business.

Where do you live? she asked.
There, I said pointing up to the third floor.
You live *there?*

There. I had to look to where she pointed--the third floor, the paint peeling, wooden bars Papa had nailed on the windows so we wouldn't fall out. You live *there?* The way she said it made me feel like nothing. *There.* I lived *there.* I nodded.

I knew then I had to have a house. A real house. One I could point to. But this isn't it. The house on Mango Street isn't it. For the time being, Mama says. Temporary, says Papa. But I know how those things go.

The House on Mango Street p. 3-5

"*A House of My Own*"

Not a flat. Not an apartment in back. Not a man's house. Not a daddy's. A house all my own. With my porch and my pillow, my pretty purple petunias. My books and my stories. My two shoes waiting beside the bed. Nobody to shake a stick at. Nobody's garbage to pick up after.

Only a house quiet as snow, a space for myself to go, clean as paper before the poem.

The House on Mango Street p. 108

"*My Name*"

In English my name means hope. In Spanish it means too many letters. It means sadness, it means waiting. It is like the number nine. A muddy color. It is the Mexican records my father plays on Sunday mornings when he is shaving, songs like sobbing.

It is my great-grandmother's name and now it is mine. She was a horse woman too, born like me in the Chinese year of the horse--which is supposed to be bad luck if you're born female--but I think this is a Chinese lie because the Chinese, like the Mexicans, don't like their women strong.

My great-grandmother. I would've liked to have known her, a wild horse of a woman, so wild she wouldn't marry. Until my great-grandfather threw a sack over her head and carried her off. Just like that, as if she were a fancy chandelier. That's the way he did it.

And the story goes she never forgave him. She looked out the window her whole life, the way so many women sit their sadness on an elbow. I wonder if she made the best of what she got or was she sorry because she couldn't be all the things she wanted to be. Esperanza. I have inherited her name, but I don't want to inherit her place by the window.

At school they say my name funny as if the syllables were made out of tin and hurt the roof of your mouth. But in Spanish my name is made out of a softer something, like silver, not quite as thick as sister's name--Magdalena--which is uglier than mine. Magdelena who at least can come home and become Nenny. But I am always Esperanza.

I would like to baptize myself under a new name, a name more like the real me, the one nobody sees. Esperanza as Lisandra or Maritza or Zeze the X. Yes. Something like Zeze the X will do.

The House on Mango Street p. 10-11

LESSON 2 LECTURE NOTES   Part B

Use the following two pages to take notes from **Part B** of the lecture. The lecture is about 11 minutes long. The information in your notes will be used to answer questions later.

_____

_____

_____

_____

_____

_____

_____

_____

_____

_____

_____

_____

_____

_____

_____

_____

_____

_____

_____

_____

_____

_____

_____

Continue Taking Notes on The Next Page

_____

_____

_____

_____

_____

_____

_____

_____

_____

_____

Lecture Question Part B.

Use your lecture notes from **Part B** to answer the following question. Use complete sentences.

What does the name Esperanza mean in English? Because Esperanza was named after her great grandmother, she is afraid. What is she afraid will happen to her in the future?

_____

_____

_____

_____

_____

_____

_____

_____

_____

Chapters (Vignettes) Dr. Sanchez refers to in Lecture Part C - Read before watching Lecture Part C

"Four Skinny Trees"

They are the only ones who understand me. I am the only one who understands them. Four skinny trees with skinny necks and pointy elbows like mine. Four who do not belong here but are here. Four raggedy excuses planted by the city. From our room we can hear them, but Nenny just sleeps and doesn't appreciate these things.

Their strength is secret. They send ferocious roots beneath the ground. They grow up and they grow down and grab the earth between their hairy toes and bite the sky with violent teeth and never quit their anger. This is how they keep.

Let one forget his reason for being, they'd all droop like tulips in a glass, each with their arms around the other. Keep, keep, keep, trees say when I sleep. They teach.

When I am too sad and too skinny to keep keeping, when I am a tiny thing against so many bricks, then it is I look at trees. When there is nothing left to look at on this street. Four who grew despite concrete. Four who reach and do not forget to reach. Four whose only reason is to be and be.

The House on Mango Street p. 74-75

"The Three Sisters"

They came with the wind that blows in August, thin as a spider web and barely noticed. Three who did not seem to be related to anything but the moon. One with laughter like tin, and one with eyes of a cat and one with hands like porcelain. The aunts, the three sisters, *las comadres*, they said.

The baby died. Lucy and Rachel's sister. One night a dog cried, and the next day a yellow bird flew in through an open window. Before the week was over, the baby's fever was worse. Then Jesus came and took the baby with him far away. That's what their mother said.

Then the visitors came...in and out of the little house. It was hard to keep the floors clean. Anybody who had ever wondered what color the walls were came and came to look at that little thumb of a human in a box like candy.

I had never seen the dead before, not for real, not in somebody's living room for people to kiss and bless themselves and light a candle for. Not in a house. It seemed strange.

They must've known, the sisters. They had the power and could sense what was what. They said, Come here, and gave me a stick of gum. They smelled like Kleenex or the inside of a satin handbag, and then I didn't feel afraid.

What's your name, the cat-eyed one asked.

Esperanza, I said.

Esperanza, the old blue-veined one repeated in a high thin voice. Esperanza...a good good name.

My knees hurt, the one with the funny laugh complained.
Tomorrow it will rain.
Yes, tomorrow, they said.

How do you know? I asked.

We know.
Look at her hands, cat-eyed said.
And they turned them over and over as if they were looking for something.
She's special.
Yes, she'll go very far.
Yes, yes, hmmm.
Make a wish.

A wish?

Yes, make a wish. What do you want?

Anything? I said.

Well, why not?

I closed my eyes.

Did you wish already?

Yes, I said.

Well, that's all there is to it. It'll come true.

How do you know? I asked.

We know, we know.

Esperanza. The one with the marble hands called me aside. Esperanza. She held my face with her blue-veined hands and looked and looked at me. A long silence. When you leave you must remember always to come back, she said.

What?

When you leave you must remember to come back for the others. A circle, understand? You will always be Esperanza. You will always be Mango Street. You can't erase what you know. You can't forget who you are.

Then I didn't know what to say. It was as if she could read my mind, as if she knew what I had wished for, and I felt ashamed for having made such a selfish wish.

You must remember to come back. For the ones who cannot leave as easily as you. You will remember? She asked as if she was telling me. Yes, yes, I said a little confused.

Good, she said rubbing my hands. Good. That's all. You can go.

I got up to join Lucy and Rachel who were already outside waiting by the door, wondering what I was doing talking to three old ladies who smelled like cinnamon. I didn't understand everything they had told me. I turned around. They smiled and waved in their smoky way.

Then I didn't see them. Not once, or twice, or ever again.

The House on Mango Street p. 103-105

"Mango Says Goodbye Sometimes"

I like to tell stories. I tell them inside my head. I tell them after the mailman says, Here's your mail. Here's your mail, he said.

I make a story for my life, for each step my brown shoe takes. I say, "And so she trudged up the wooden stairs, her sad brown shoes taking her to the house she never liked."

I like to tell stories. I am going to tell you a story about a girl who didn't want to belong.

We didn't always live on Mango Street. Before that we lived on Loomis on the third floor, and before that we lived on Keeler. Before Keeler it was Paulina, but what I remember most is Mango Street, sad red house, the house I belong but do not belong to.

I put it down on paper and then the ghost does not ache so much. I write it down and Mango says goodbye sometimes. She does not hold me with both arms. She sets me free.

One day I will pack my bags of books and paper. One day I will say goodbye to Mango. I am too strong for her to keep me forever. One day I will go away.

Friends and neighbors will say, What happened to that Esperanza? Where did she go with all those books and paper? Why did she march so far away?

They will not know I have gone away to come back. For the ones I left behind. For the ones who cannot out.

The House on Mango Street p. 109-110

LESSON 2 LECTURE NOTES   Part C

Use the following two pages to take notes from **Part C** of the lecture. This part of the lecture is about 11 minutes long. The information in your notes will be used to answer a question later.

_____

_____

_____

_____

_____

_____

_____

_____

_____

_____

_____

_____

_____

_____

_____

_____

_____

_____

_____

_____

_____

_____

Continue Taking Notes on The Next Page

_____

_____

_____

_____

_____

_____

_____

_____

_____

_____

_____

_____

Lecture Question Part C

Use your lecture notes from **Part C** to answer the following question. Use complete sentences.

> **After Esperanza makes a wish to leave Mango Street, one of the mysterious women tells her, "When you leave you must remember to come back for the others, a circle, understand?" Explain what it means for Esperanza to "come back" and how she will do this in her future.**

_____

_____

_____

_____

_____

_____

_____

_____

_____

_____

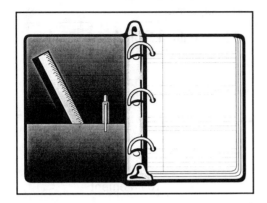

Lecture Signals -

Dr. Reuben Sanchez

We saw in Lesson 1 (Dr. Tanner) that lectures have a structure or organization. The professor gives you signals about what is important to write down. When you are reading, these signals about what is important are indicated by titles, subtitles, paragraph breaks, bolding, and also by some of the same signals professors use when they speak. In lectures, you can't see the signals like you can in reading. Since professors speak so quickly and so much during a college course, you need to practice listening for the signals about what is important to write down. In Lesson 1 we organized lecture signals into the following categories:

Lecture Signals

Signal Category	Explanation	Example
I. Topic Marker	tells you what the topic is	Today's lecture is on... The next issue we will discuss is...
II. Checkpoint Marker	tells you where the professor is in a lecture or when the professor is changing to a new topic or concluding the lecture	
A. Topic Shifter	may be an aside - almost spoken to himself/herself at the end of a particular point	Now... OK.... Let's see... Right... Alright...
B. Concluder	signals end of topic or end of lecture	That's what you need to know about... That covers the topic of...
III. Information Expander	these are important signals that give the following kinds of information:	
A. Give background information	gives the historical or social context	As you may remember from history... During this time period we also saw...
B. Explain meaning	gives a definition or restatement of the topic or idea	In other words... By this I mean...
C. Give an example	could also be anecdote (little personal story) or joke	For example... In the real world this would be... In terms of...
D. Relate two pieces of information:	often uses "Connector" words and phrases (see vocabulary section)	

1. **Cause-effect**	how "A" causes "B" to happen	The result of this is... This causes the following to happen...
2. **Contrast**	how are "A" and "B" different	In contrast... On the other hand... The opposite is true for...
3. **Compare**	how are "A" and "B" the same	All three men believe... Similarly...
IV. Information Qualifier	gives a different value to the information	
A. **Emphasize importance of information**	draws your attention to the important points in the lecture	repetition, restatement
1. **Rhetorical question***	a question asked of the whole class - no answer is expected	What do you think he did next? What do you think the answer is?
2. **Imperative***	an "order" to the students	Remember this. Write this down.
3. **Direct statement of importance**	the professor tells you directly how important something is	This is important. Pay particular attention to this point.
B. **Information Corrector**	professor made a mistake and is correcting himself/herself	Oh, what I meant to say was...
C. **Emphasize information is not very important**	extra information you don't have to write down - added to make the lecture more interesting	This may not be relevant but... By the way...
V. Summarizer	professor will summarize or restate the important information	In summary...As I said before... In other words...

* rhetorical question - When someone asks a rhetorical question, he or she expects no answer. It is just a question that guides the lecture or conversation. For example, when you are driving, you may ask about a driver in front of you, "What is that crazy guy doing?" You really don't expect anyone in the car to answer this rhetorical question.

* imperative sentence - This kind of sentence is like an order. You are telling someone what to do. The sentence usually starts with a verb: Bring me the book. Open the window. The professor is telling you to focus your attention on something: Consider the following.

→ **TASK:** Read the following signals that Dr. Sanchez gave you during the lecture. Discuss their meaning as a whole class.

Dr. Sanchez said:	Lecture Signal:	Meaning:
1. ... that is what I am going to talk to you about today	I. Topic Marker	write this down
2. But first there are a couple of terms we need to talk about to begin with.	III. Information Expander A. Background	gives necessary background vocabulary for the lecture
3. We can refer to them as vignettes.	III. Information Expander B. Explain meaning	definition of the concept
4. You have the child's wished-for escape on the one hand and you have the writer's self-empowered return on the other.	III. Information Expander D. Relate 2 Information 2. Contrast	the contrast is an important point in the lecture
5. There we are presented with one of the central problems in the text.	IV. Information Qualifier A. Emphasize importance 3. Direct statement	the central problem is the most important problem - write this down
6. She will know it by the end of the book. Now how does she know it?	IV. Information Qualifier A. Emphasize importance 1. Rhetorical question	how she knows it is an important point - he is drawing your attention to this with the rhetorical question
7. So that is what I mean when I say we must distinguish author from character in the book.	V. Summarizer	summarizes the point he was making during the past few minutes
8. We could spend a lot more time talking about this book, but unfortunately, we can't do that.	II. Checkpoint Marker B. Concluder	signals end of lecture

Practice 1

➜ **TASK:** The following list includes more signals Dr. Sanchez used during his lecture. Work in small groups to decide what kind of signal each is and indicate the kind of signal and the meaning of the signal in the space provided. Check your answers with the whole class as you discuss each signal and see if you agree with the other groups.

Dr. Sanchez said:	Lecture Signal:	Meaning:
1. Novel is a very generalized term. It is basically a long work of fiction.		
2. Another term we want to talk about is protagonist.		
3. So again, the idea of place is very important in this book.		
4. The idea of writer is an image or symbol of one's place in the world.		
5. I think it is a very important vignette.		
6. There are basically two different points of view that an author presents a text in.		
7. Now when we talk about the narrator we also talk about tone of voice.		
8. To keep from being abducted, what does it take?		
9. To survive you have to be angry and that of course ties into Esperanza's desire not to be overwhelmed like her great grandmother.		
10. They have a childlike quality but that doesn't mean that they are simple stories.		

Practice 2 - Note-taking Skills Practice

→ **TASK:**   Symbols and Abbreviations Review. Fill in the blank with the appropriate symbol or abbreviation. Use the abbreviations list in Lesson 1 if you can't remember these.

Word(s)	Abbrev./Symbol	Word(s)	Abbrev./Symbol
at		for example	
without		that is	
versus		not applicable	
not equal		approximately	
greater than		therefore	
with		less than	

Some New Abbreviations: These abbreviations are common in textbooks. You may want to use them when you take notes.

Abbreviation   **Meaning**

c.   short for *circa*, which means approximately for dates, when the date is not sure. For example, "He was born c. 1650."

re   short for the Latin phrase *in re*, which means about this topic. For example, "Re your letter of January 5, 1995, I will not be able to attend the meeting you invited me to."

B. Reading Note-taking and Summarizing

→ **TASK:**   You will be taking notes from two sections of reading about Sandra Cisneros and her novel. Be sure to use symbols and abbreviations in your notes and try to say things in your own words. Don't copy from the reading! You may use the dictionary at the end of the lesson if you want to look up any words. You will also be writing summaries of the of the information you took notes on.

TEXTBOOK READING PART 1 Underline the important information as you read.
Take notes on the information in the box.

About the author

Sandra Cisneros was born in Chicago in 1954. She has worked as a teacher to high school dropouts, a poet-in-the-schools, a college recruiter, and an arts administrator. Most recently, she has taught as a visiting writer at a number of universities around the country. The recipient of two NEA fellowships for poetry and fiction, Cisneros is the author of *Woman Hollering Creek* (Random House), a collection of stories, and *My Wicked Wicked Ways* (Third Woman), a volume of poetry.

The daughter of a Mexican father and a Mexican-American mother, and sister to six brothers, she is nobody's mother and nobody's wife. She currently lives in San Antonio, Texas.

--From *About the Author*
The House on Mango Street

Cultural Perspective

Sandra Cisneros writes from the point of view of the culture she grew up in, the inner-city Hispanic barrio or ghetto of Chicago. Culture shapes the way we think; it tells us what "makes sense." It holds people together by providing us with a shared set of customs, values, ideas, and beliefs, as well as a common language. We live enmeshed in this cultural web: it influences the way we relate to others, the way we dress, our tastes, our habits. But as culture binds us together, it also selectively blinds us. As we grow up, we accept ways of looking at the world, ways of thinking and being that might be best characterized as cultural frames of reference or cultural myths. Thus, although Esperanza wanted a house of her own away from Mango Street, she realized that she would always return to Mango Street or her cultural perspective and roots.

--adapted from *Prereading America*, p.3

The Bildungsroman

Dr. Sanchez classifies *The House on Mango Street* as a Bildungsroman. This kind of book is usually about the personal development of a single individual.

Bildungsroman (German word meaning "novel of educational formation" or "education novel") is a class of novel developed in German literature that deals with the formative years of an individual up to his arrival at a man's estate and a responsible place in society. It is sometimes called an Entwicklungsroman ("novel of character development"). The form was especially popular between 1790 and 1860.

Perhaps the chief examples in English are Charles Dickens' *David Copperfield* (1849-50) and James Joyce's *A Portrait of the Artist as a Young Man* (1916).

A story about the emergence of a personality and a talent, with its implicit motifs of struggle, conflict, suffering, and success, has an inevitable appeal for the novelist; many first novels are autobiographical and attempt to generalize the author's own adolescent experiences into a kind of universal symbol of the growing and learning processes.

-- adapted from the *Encyclopedia Britannica* and *Grolier's Encyclopedia*

Reading Note-taking Part 1:

Take notes on the reading section in the box. Use abbreviations. Don't copy sentences from the reading.

_____

_____

_____

_____

_____

_____

_____

_____

_____

_____

Reading Summary Part 1:

Write a summary of the section in the box. Use your own words.

_____

_____

_____

_____

_____

_____

_____

_____

_____

_____

_____

Reviews of the Book

"Told in a series of vignettes stunning for their eloquence, THE HOUSE ON MANGO STREET is the story of Esperanza Cordero, a young girl growing up in the Hispanic quarter of Chicago. For Esperanza, Mango Street is a desolate landscape of concrete and run-down tenements, where she discovers the hard realities of life--the fetters of class and gender, the specter of racial enmity, the mysteries of sexuality, and more. Capturing her thoughts and emotions in poems and stories, Esperanza is able to rise above hopelessness, and create for herself "a house all my own...quiet as snow, a space for myself to go," in the midst of her oppressive surroundings.

Brilliantly evocative, hauntingly lyrical, intensely compelling, THE HOUSE ON MANGO STREET signals the emergence of a major new literary talent."

--From the book jacket

On the Reading Process

If a reader has little background knowledge, a text may appear incomprehensible. A writer provides only as much detail as the reader needs, relying on the stored knowledge of the reader in order to fill in the gaps left vacant in the text. For this reason, it is always easier to understand the material you are reading if you have some background information about the topic or the themes of the writing.

To fully understand Cisneros' writing about the inner-city in Chicago from a child's point of view, it would be helpful to understand something about the history of the Mexican immigrant population in that city.

It would also be helpful to understand something about the author's family background because the book is described as a semi-autobiographical work which is explicitly feminist, or at least has had considerable impact upon the feminist community. Feminism is a perspective or belief system that advocates political, economic, and social equality of the sexes, and therefore often is organized around activity on behalf of women's rights and interests.

The Genre of the Western Novel

The Western novel is a product of modern civilization, although in the Far East novels began separate development as early as the 10th century. Extended prose works of complex interpersonal relations and motivations begin in 17th-century France. Eighteenth-century France produced an immense number of novels dealing with love analysis. For example, Pierre Choderlos de Laclos wrote *Les Liaisons Dangereuses* (1782), made into a film in 1993 (*Dangerous Liaisons*) starring Glenn Close and Michelle Pfeiffer.

The 19th century was the golden age of the novel. It became ever more profound, complex, and subtle (or, on the other hand, more popular, eventful, and sentimental). By the beginning of the 20th century it had become the most common form of thoughtful reading matter and had replaced, for most educated people, religious, philosophical, and scientific works as a medium for the interpretation of life.

By the late 1920s the novel had begun to show signs of decay as a form, and no works have since been produced to compare with the recent past. This may be a temporarily barren period, or else the novel may be losing its energy as a narrative art form and in this sense giving way to the medium of film.

--adapted from *Encyclopedia Britannica* 10, p. 1048

Reading Note-taking Part 2:

Take notes on the reading section in the box. Use abbreviations. Don't copy sentences from the reading.

_____

_____

_____

_____

_____

_____

_____

_____

_____

_____

_____

Reading Summary Part 2:

Write a summary of the section in the box. Use your own words.

_____

_____

_____

_____

_____

_____

_____

_____

_____

_____

_____

_____

2. Academic Vocabulary Building

Word Attack Skills: The more you know about word roots and endings (prefixes and suffixes), the easier it will be to read and learn new words.

Review from Lesson 1: Work with a partner or in a small group to complete these review exercises. If you need to, you can look back to lesson 1 for help.

Practice 3 Prefix Review

➡ **TASK:**   **Prefixes:** Explain the meaning of each prefix from Lesson 1 and give an example of a word that uses this prefix.

Prefix	Meaning	Example
1. pre-	_____	_____
2. dis-	_____	_____
3. con-	_____	_____
4. un-	_____	_____
5. ir-	_____	_____

Practice 4 Suffix Review

➡ **TASK:**   Explain the meaning of each suffix from Lesson 1, indicate whether the suffix is a noun, adjective, or verb ending, and give an example of word that has this suffix, and give a definition of the word.

Suffix	Word Form	Example	Definition
1. -bility	_____	_____	_____
2. -ize	_____	_____	_____
3. -ist	_____	_____	_____
4. -able	_____	_____	_____
5. -ism	_____	_____	_____
6. -ful	_____	_____	_____
7. -ology	_____	_____	_____

Practice 5 Roots Review

➡ **TASK:**   Explain the meaning of the roots you studied in Lesson 1, give an example of a word that has this root, and explain the meaning of the example.

Root	Meaning	Example	Definition
1. sume, sumpt	_____	_____	_____
2. dic, dict	_____	_____	_____
3. psyche	_____	_____	_____
4. cogn	_____	_____	_____
5. sequ	_____	_____	_____
6. matur	_____	_____	_____

Roots Used in Lesson 2

Root	Meaning	Examples
spect	look	perspective, specter
sci	know	science, omniscience, conscience (note pronunciation differences for the last two words - "sh" sound)
fict	invent, form	fiction, fictional, fictitious
loqu, locu	speak	colloquial, eloquence, circumlocution, locution
graph	write	biography, autobiography
arm	weapons	army, disarming
liter	letter, writing	literature, literary, literate, literal
patri, pater	father	patriarchal, paternal, paternity
arch	chief	patriarch, monarch, archetype, archetypical
matri, mater	mother	matriarchal, maternal, maternity
sume, sumpt	take, take up	presume, assume, resume
viv	live	survive, survival, revive, vivid
fem, femina	woman	feminine, feminism, female
soph	wise	philosopher, sophisticated
phil	love	philosopher, philharmonic,
voc	call, voice	vocation, advocate, vocal, evoke
bio	life	biography, biology, biochemist
vis	see	television, visual, visit

Prefixes Used in Lesson 2

Prefix	Meaning	Examples
omni	all	omniscient, omnivore, omnipresent
en	in	enmesh, enshrine, encircle, enslave, enfold
cent	hundred	century, centigrade, centimeter
auto	self	autobiography, automobile, automatic
circ	ring	circle, circular, circulate
dis	not	disarming
em	in	empower
in	not	informal, incomprehensible
re	again	resume
pre	before	presume, presumably, presumption
per	throughout	perspective, pervasive, perpetual
inter	between, among	interpersonal
ad	to	advocate
con	with	conscience
semi	half; partly	semi-autobiographical; semi-automatic

Important Prefix Pairs

Some prefixes can be learned in pairs that have opposite meanings.

between, among = **inter**	≠	**intra, intro** = within
outside, beyond = **extra**	≠	**intro, intra** = within
small = **micro, mini**	≠	**macro, maxi, mega** = large (mega also=1 million)
before = **pre**	≠	**post** = after
same = **homo**	≠	**hetero** = different
for = **pro**	≠	**contra, anti** = against
good = **bene**	≠	**mal, dys** = bad
over, above = **super, supra**	≠	**sub, subter** = under, below
over, beyond, extra = **hyper**	≠	**hypo** = under, too little

Practice 6 Prefix   Pairs Practice

→ **TASK** Use the prefix pairs above to explain the words below.

1. Delta is an international airline.

    international _____

2. Intrastate truck companies carry most of California's agricultural products from the farms to Los Angeles.

    intrastate   _____

3. She is an extraordinary teacher.

    extraordinary _____

4. The new computers have very fast microchips.

    microchip   _____

5. It was a ten megaton bomb.

    megaton   _____

6. Lesson 1 uses your pretest results.

    pretest   _____

7. After you finish the lesson there will be a posttest.

    posttest   _____

8. Some people are homosexual.

   homosexual _____

9. Some people are heterosexual.

   heterosexual _____

10. Some people are pro-abortion rights.

    pro-abortion _____

11. Some people are anti-abortion.

    anti-abortion _____

12. Spoiled food is malodorous.

    malodorous _____

13. Some people are dysfunctional.

    dysfunctional _____

14. Ms. McClay is my supervisor.

    supervisor _____

15. The cars were recalled by the manufacturer because they had substandard seatbelts.

    substandard _____

16. He is a hyperactive child.

    hyperactive _____

17. You should not stay in cold water for a long time because of the danger of hypothermia.

    hypothermia _____
    (therm means temperature - as in thermometer)

Suffixes Lesson 2

Person Suffixes In Lesson 1 you learned the suffix -ist meaning the person who does something or specializes in something (theorist, psychologist). Here is a list of suffixes that indicate a person who does something.

-ist	novelist, protagonist
-er, -or	teacher, professor
-eer	engineer
-ier	financier

-ster	gangster
-ine	female ending - heroine Esperanza is the protagonist or heroine.
-trix	female ending - aviatrix (not very common)
-ess	female ending - actress, waitress

Vocabulary Building

Practice 7   Trick Word Matching Exercise

➜ **TASK:**   As you remember from Lesson 1, words or phrases that have a ✔ after them may have a different meaning from the common meaning when used in an academic context. Work in small groups to check your knowledge of the Trick Words from Lesson 1 and the new Trick Words in Lesson 2. Match the Trick Words with the correct definition of the word as it is used in the lecture or textbook for these two lessons.

Lesson 1 Trick Words ✔   **Definition**

bare my soul _____	1. do something, participate in something
discipline _____	2. type of academic work, field
recognize _____	3. way to do something, study something
field _____	4. tell you my secret thoughts
engage in _____	5. understand, accept that something is correct
approach _____	6. area of study or work

Lesson 2 Trick Words ✔   **Definitions**

conception _____	1. beginning, first
dig more deeply _____	2. not easily forgotten, always remembered
feminism _____	3. seems simple, without complication or suspicion
disarming _____	4. a short piece of writing
quality _____	5. a certain part of the city
voice _____	6. the formal or informal tone used in writing
passage _____	7. a kind of apartment
works _____	8. the characteristic or nature of something
fellowship _____	9. idea, understanding
quarter _____	10. belief in equal rights for women
initial _____	11. standards, what people think are right or wrong
flat _____	12. the writing, art, or music someone produces
hauntingly _____	13. the money you get to study or do academic work
values _____	14. try to understand better, think more
roots _____	15. writing from Europe, western hemisphere, not East
Western novel _____	16. ancestors, family background

Practice 8 Noun Forms of Adjectives

➜ **TASK:** Academic language uses more noun forms of words than does the language we speak with friends. It is important to learn the noun forms of all the new words you study in each lesson. For the adjectives listed below, write their noun form. You can use the dictionary at the end of the lesson if you need to.

Adjective	Noun Form	Adjective	Noun Form
1. deep	_____	24. desolate	_____
2. omniscient	_____	25. colloquial	_____
3. mysterious	_____	26. relevant	_____
4. precise	_____	27. barren	_____
5. profound	_____	28. extended	_____
6. valid	_____	29. patriarchal	_____
7. adolescent	_____	30. formative	_____
8. ambitious	_____	31. inevitable	_____
9. empowered	_____	32. oppressive	_____
10. ferocious	_____	33. significant	_____
11. incomprehensible	_____	34. motivated	_____
12. symbolic	_____	35. confused	_____
13. intimate	_____	36. eloquent	_____
14. received	_____	37. wise	_____
15. philosophical	_____	38. fictional	_____
16. sentimental	_____	39. emerging	_____
17. simplistic	_____	40. inherited	_____
18. sophisticated	_____	41. dominated	_____
19. subtle	_____	42. societal	_____
20. central	_____	43. potential	_____
21. ideal	_____		
22. harsh	_____		
23. immense	_____		

Practice 9 Lesson 2 Nouns

➜ **TASK:**   The following words are noun forms from the Lesson 2 lecture or reading. Match each noun with its definition listed below and on the next page. Work in small groups. Use the Lesson 2 Dictionary if necessary.

Thinking

conflict _____
confusion _____
myths _____
perspective _____

Person Characteristics

ambition _____
eloquence _____
enmity _____
enthusiasm _____
heroine _____
maturity _____
motivation _____
protagonist _____
role _____
soul _____
vocation _____

Importance   significance _____

Information

medium _____
symbol _____
theme _____

Research, Academic

dissertation _____
genre _____
prose _____
specialization _____
vignette _____

Cause-Effect, Change

decay _____
emergence _____
impact _____
recipient _____

History, Government, Society

barrio _____
ghetto _____
recruiter _____
society _____

Time

century _____
gap _____

Definitions

1. cause change, affect
2. your goals in life, what you want
3. writing similar to everyday speech, not poetry
4. beautiful speaking or writing, words
5. person who tries to get others to join
6. coming out, appearance
7. a kind or form of writing
8. the field or area you know most about
9. interest, positive support, excitement
10. importance
11. the culture we live in, the people in the culture
12. decline, dying out, falling apart
13. empty space, missing information
14. point of view, the way you think about something
15. the person who receives something
16. neighborhood (in Spanish)
17. slum, poor area of town, bad housing
18. reaching adult age
19. the main character who is a female
20. job, profession, occupation
21. research to complete Ph.D. degree
22. traditional stories
23. hostility, active hatred
24. thing or picture that represents something else
25. short piece of writing (French)
26. person or the spiritual part of the person, not body
27. the main story, main idea
28. main character of a story
29. what you do, or part played by actor
30. one hundred years
31. the reason you do something
32. no understanding, poor thinking
33. a way of passing information, like tv, books
34. disagreement, argument, struggle

Practice 10 Lesson 2 Verbs

→ **TASK:**   The following are verbs from the Lesson 2 lecture or reading. Explain the
meaning of each verb and **use it in a sentence**. Work in small groups and read
your answers to the whole class.

1. identify with _____

_____

2. realize _____

_____

3. narrate _____

_____

4. generalize _____

_____

5. symbolize _____

_____

6. fulfill _____

_____

7. advocate _____

_____

8. baptize _____

_____

9. inherit _____

_____

10. simplify _____

_____

Practice 11   Word Attack ✂ ✂ ✂ ✂

➜ **TASK:**   The following words can be explained by breaking them apart and looking at all the prefixes, suffixes, and roots. Work in small groups to pull the words apart. Be prepared to explain to the class how you pulled them apart.

1. semi-autobiographical _____

   _____

2. omniscient _____

   _____

3. empower _____

   _____

4. advocate _____

   _____

5. presume _____

   _____

6. perspective_____

   _____

7. century _____

   _____

8. disarming _____

   _____

9. informal _____

   _____

10. patriarch _____

   _____

11. nonfiction _____

   _____

12. conscience_____

   _____

13. extracurricular _____

   _____

14. semiliterate _____

   _____

15. philosophy _____

   _____

16. revive _____

   _____

17. matriarchy _____

   _____

18. sophisticated _____

   _____

19. intrastate _____

   _____

20. interstate _____

_____

21. posttest _____

_____

22. contradict _____

_____

Practice 12 Word Endings

→ **TASK**   The following are excerpts from Dr. Sanchez' lecture. The endings have been removed from some of the vocabulary words you have been studying. Work in small groups to fill in the blanks with the correct word endings. In order to do this exercise you need to determine what word form is being used in the sentence (noun, verb, adjective, adverb). In some cases, NO ending needs to be added because the word is correct as it is written.

1. The novel is a very generaliz____ term.

2. It is basic____ a long work of fiction____ that is writ____ in prose____ .

3. A Bildungsroman is a novel of educat____ or form____.

4. It is a story about a young____ person who____ is mov____ from child____ to matur____.

5. The story concern___ some initial___ state of confus____.

6. The central character____ moves to some kind of aware____ or understand_____.

7. Mango Street is part of her identi____, but she want____ to escap____.

8. Esperanza will come back, maybe not literal___, but symbolic____ through her writ____.

9. The significan____ of wanting to leave and needing to come back is our percept____ of the

conflict.

10. Her great grandmother lived in a patriarch____ societ____ that kept the female____

in the tradition____ female role____.

11. It make____ use of colloqu____ language and therefore may appear____ simpl____

or unsophistic____.

12. It is a very deep____ and profound____ text that is worth
read____.

I LOVE VOCABULARY

3. Reading

Reading Strategies Lesson 2:

Underlining Text

In college, you have to do a lot of reading in each class you take. Most students underline or highlight as they read so they can look back later at the text and just find the important information. If they underline carefully, they don't have to read everything again; they just read the underlined parts. When you have underlined carefully, taking notes from the reading is much easier. In college, you need notes from your reading to write papers, answer test questions, and to help study for exams.

When you practice looking for the important information and underlining it in these lessons, you should learn to underline the right parts of the sentence. If you only underline a few words, it won't mean anything to you when you try to go back and read again. If you underline too much, you will be reading the whole text again. If you underline the wrong things, you can even change the meaning of the passage. For example, if you underline the verb, but forget to underline the word NOT, you won't know that the sentence is negative. There is an example of this below.

Here is an example of a student who did not underline enough. Try reading just the parts that are underlined. Do you see why it is a problem to underline too little?

Sandra Cisneros' book *The House on Mango Street* was discovered by a large publishing firm, Random House, in <u>1991</u>. It had originally been published in <u>1984</u> by a small press at the <u>University of Houston</u>. This college publishing firm devotes its entire catalog to minority writers of Latin American origin who write in English. Even though it was not <u>popular at its first printing</u>, *The House on Mango Street* eventually became a "hot item" among publishers for three reasons: First and most important, it's written by a <u>Mexican-American woman</u>. Second, it uses words and expressions that paint pictures which are <u>typical among Hispanics</u> of Aztec origin. And third, it is a very easy book to read. (Adapted from *Una Nueva Voz*, 13 September 1991)

Here is an example of a student who underlined too much. Do you see the problem with underlining almost everything? You have to make a judgment about each sentence as you read and decide if it is important to underline.

Sandra <u>Cisneros' book *The House on Mango Street* was discovered by</u> a large publishing firm, <u>Random House, in 1991</u>. It had <u>originally been published in 1984 by a small press at the University of Houston</u>. <u>This college publishing firm devotes its entire catalog to minority writers of Latin American origin who write in English</u>. <u>Even though it was not popular at its first printing, *The House on Mango Street* eventually became a "hot item" among publishers for three reasons: First and most important, it's written by a Mexican-American woman. Second, it uses words and expressions that paint pictures which are typical</u> among Hispanics of Aztec origin. And <u>third, it is a very easy book to read</u>. (Adapted from *Una Nueva Voz*, 13 September 1991)

➡ **Practice 13 TASK:**   Work together is small groups or with the whole class to decide what should be underlined in this passage.

Sandra Cisneros' book *The House on Mango Street* was discovered by a large publishing firm, Random House, in 1991. It had originally been published in 1984 by a small press at the University of Houston. This college publishing firm devotes its entire catalog to minority writers of Latin American origin who write in English. Even though it was not popular at its first printing, *The House on Mango Street* eventually became a "hot item" among publishers for three reasons: First and most important, it's written by a Mexican-American woman. Second, it uses words and expressions that paint pictures which are typical among Hispanics of Aztec origin. And third, it is a very easy book to read. (Adapted from *Una Nueva Voz*, 13 September 1991)

More Underlining Strategies: Here are some other strategies you can use to help you get control over the text you are reading

1. Use different colors for your underlining or highlighting. One color could indicate a definition, another color could be used for the most important information, a third color could be used to indicate the first time a new topic is introduced.
2. Use note-taking abbreviations and symbols in the margins to remind you what you have read. A star could mean the most important information, **def** could mean definition, **ex** could mean example, etc.

 Develop your own personal strategies that work for you when you read for information!

Self-monitoring: Metacognitive Strategies

The reading you do in college can be difficult. In college you are reading to learn new information, to write papers, and to prepare for exams. This is not like the reading you have done on 'Reading Tests' where you may have skimmed through a paragraph to look for the piece of information to answer the question. It is also not like the reading you may have done to answer questions in high school textbooks. In college you have to read a lot, take notes from the reading, and be able to answer questions based on all of the reading. The textbook reading will also help you understand the professor's lecture, but the professor usually gives you new information that is not in the textbook and just expects that you have already read the textbook.

In order to be successful in doing college reading you need to practice some new reading strategies. You have already practiced looking for important information and crossing out unimportant information (Lesson 1). In this lesson you will also practice looking for the important information and underlining it. In addition, you will practice self-monitoring strategies. These are the strategies good readers use when they come to something they have trouble understanding.

All readers (even your teacher and professors) finds themselves facing some reading that they have trouble understanding. Besides learning new vocabulary, as you are doing in these lessons, you can also learn self-monitoring or *metacognitive* strategies. We will practice these strategies as a group so that you can practice them by yourself when you have difficult reading to do. Reading teachers refer to these strategies as metacognition or metacomprehension. The prefix *meta-* means *beyond*. So metacognition means beyond thinking, or thinking about your thinking process. Dr. Tanner spoke about this is Lesson 1. Metacomprehension means thinking about your own reading comprehension. In other words, you should always be thinking about whether you understand what you are reading <u>while</u> you are reading.

Metacomprehension Practice: A Class "Think Aloud".

Self-monitoring means you keep checking yourself to see how you are doing - that's what good readers do. Metacomprehension consists of two main self-monitoring tasks. First, the reader (you) should always ask what you think the author is trying to say **before** you read and **while** you read. Second, you should always ask yourself what you are thinking and how well you understand **while** you are reading. You are going to practice these strategies in a 'think-aloud' exercise with the whole class.

Passage for Class Think-Aloud

Mexican Immigration to Chicago: The First Wave

Labor Shortages

Mexican immigration into the Chicago area reached large and steady proportions in 1916-1929 as a direct result of labor imports by Midwest and Chicago-area employers. A war-related economic boom coincided with a sharp decline of European migration, resulting in labor shortages, particularly in low-wage occupations and industries, as domestic workers moved into better paying opportunities.

The Role of the Railroads and Seasonal Work

The railroads imported Mexican workers for track labor in 1916. Recruitment continued steadily and by 1928, Mexicans constituted 43% of the track and maintenance workers on 16 major railroads in the Chicago region. Sugar beet companies also imported Mexicans during and after World War I for seasonal work. After the season, however, many of these workers were enticed by urban employers to enter Chicago and other Midwest cities for higher wages and year-round employment.

Other Industries

The successful experience of the railroads was soon imitated by other industries in the Chicago area, particularly during the strikes of the steel (1919) and meat-packing industries (1921). By 1926, 14% of the workforce employed in steel in the Chicago area was Mexican and by 1928, 11% of the workers in meat-packing were Mexican. As a result of these importation efforts, with the exception of the 1921-1922 recession, the Mexican population in Chicago increased steadily during this period from 1,224 in 1920 to 19,362 in 1930.

Adapted from *Latinos in a Changing U.S. Economy*, Morales, R. and Bonilla, F., Editors, 1993.

A. Pre-reading

- What is this about? (Look at the titles and subtitles).
- What do you know about the passage just from reading the subtitles?
- What do you already know about this topic?

Thinking about what you know already will help you understand what you are reading. It is always easier to understand a topic if you know a little about it before you start reading. Without reading anything else except the two subtitles, discuss with the whole class what they already know about Mexican immigration, Chicago, World War II, and the word 'wave' as it is used here.

B. Pre-reading

•   What kinds of information will I see in this writing?

As a group, make predictions about what kinds of information you will probably find in this passage. Do not read anything except the subtitles before you make these predictions.

C. Pre-reading

•   Why am I reading this and what will I do with the information?

If this is a college assignment, you will want to underline the important information and probably take notes. In this exercise you will be underlining the important information and you will decide sentence by sentence with the class what should be underlined.

D. During Reading Each sentence should be read out loud one at a time by different students. Ask the following questions as you read:

1. How well did I understand this sentence? (Be honest!)

2. Are there any vocabulary words I am not sure of? If so, can I guess the meaning (see word attack skills, Lesson 1).

3. Can I break this sentence into smaller parts or shorter sentences? (see sentence complexity exercises in each lesson).

4. Can I explain what this sentence means in my own words?

5. Should any of this be underlined because it is important information?

6. What is going to come next in the passage?

Example of applying these 6 question to the first sentence in the passage:

Mexican immigration into the Chicago area reached large and steady proportions in 1916-1929 as a direct result of labor imports by Midwest and Chicago-area employers.

1. **How well did I understand this sentence?** Answer this honestly as either:
   a) I understand it well,
   b) I sort of understand, or
   c) I really don't understand it.

2. **Are there any vocabulary words I am not sure of?** Discuss as a class each of these words or phrases.

Mexican	immigration
Chicago area	steady proportions
as a direct result	labor
imports	Midwest
employers	

3. **Can I break this sentence into smaller parts or shorter sentences?**

Mexican immigration into the Chicago area reached large and steady proportions in 1916-1929 as a direct result of labor imports by Midwest and Chicago-area employers.

- Mexicans immigrated to the Chicago area.
- A lot immigrated during 1916 to 1929.
- They immigrated because of Midwest and Chicago-area employers.
- The employers needed workers or labor for their businesses.

4. **Can I explain what this sentence means in my own words?** Students can volunteer to try to restate or explain this sentence in their own words.

5. **Should any of this be underlined because it is important information?**

Yes. Discuss as a class what to underline. You should probably underline these points: Mexican immigration / Chicago/ large / 1916-1929 / labor imports. This captures the most important information and leaves out what is less important.

6. **What is going to come next in the passage?** Make predictions about what is coming next. You can do this by asking questions.

Why did Mexicans immigrate?

Why did employers need workers?

Why was this time period of 1916-1929 important?

How did employers get Mexicans to immigrate to Chicago and the Midwest?

→ **TASK:**   Apply the same 6 questions to each sentence in a whole class think-aloud exercise for the entire passage.

---

5. Post-reading. Close the book and as a whole class 'reconstruct' the passage on the black board. Try to remember the subtitles and the important information in the passage. If you can't remember much, you did not really understand the passage and your self-monitoring was not working.

☞ *Apply these pre-reading, during-reading, and post-reading steps to everything you read!*

4. Sentence Complexity

More Conditional Sentences In Lesson 1 you practiced 'pulling apart' and constructing sentences that used "if ... then" or conditional constructions. If you need to review that lesson before doing this lesson, go back and spend a few minutes reviewing.

Practice 14   Conditional Sentence Practice

→ **TASK** The following are conditional sentences from the Lesson 2 reading and lecture. For each sentence, break it down into smaller sentences and decide whether it is a one-way or two-way conditional sentence.

From the Reading:

1. For this reason, it is always easier to understand the material you are reading if you have some background information about the topic or the themes of the writing.

From the Lecture:

2. Cisneros is making the argument that anger can be something positive if it helps you survive in the world.

3. So even if you leave, you are going to take Mango Street with you.

98

Nominalization   Verb ➜ Noun

One way academic writing is different from the English we speak is that is uses more nouns. Often these academic sentences are formed by taking the verb and making it into a noun. For example, in the following sentence, **development** and **formation** (noun forms) are used instead of the verbs **develop** and **form**.

The Bildungsroman includes the **development** of the individual and the **formation** of the individual's mind.

This could have been written as follows:

In the Bildungsroman, the individual **develops** and his mind **forms**.

Practice 15   Nominalization

➜ **TASK:**   One way you can learn to understand long complex academic sentences is to find the nouns and see if you change them back into verbs (not all nouns have a verb form) and then make smaller sentences (with the verbs) out of the long sentences. The following are nominalized sentences from the Lesson 2 reading or lecture. Break these sentences into shorter sentences and change the nouns that are in **bold type** back into verbs.

Example: The Western novel is a **product** of modern civilization, although in the Far East novels began separate **development** as early as the 10th century.

Modern civilization **produced** the Western novel.
However, novels **developed** separately as early as the 10th century in the Far East.

1. Cisneros worked as a **teacher** to high school dropouts and as a college **recruiter**.

2. She is the **recipient** of two fellowships.

3. A story about the **emergence** of a personality that had **struggle** and **suffering** has inevitable **appeal** for the novelist.

4. The novel is about Esperanza's initial **confusion** and her later **understanding** of life.

5. Academic Culture

Institutions and Degrees:

Higher education refers to education after high school (also known as secondary school). Thus higher education is also called postsecondary education (post=after).

Community College

Community colleges (formerly called junior colleges, sometimes called city colleges) are institutions that provide the first two years of a four-year college education and/or provide students who graduate with an A.A. (Associate of Arts) degree.

Many community college students transfer to a four year college to complete their four-year or bachelor's degree. Students receive either a Bachelor of Science (B.S.) degree or Bachelor of Arts (B.A. or sometimes A.B.) degree, depending on their major. Major is the field of study emphasized during the college education. For example, some students major in psychology, biology, or history.

The term four-year institution distinguishes colleges and universities from community colleges, which are termed two-year institutions. However, the four-year term is no longer really correct because it often takes students five or even six years to complete their bachelor's degree requirements and graduate.

The bachelor's degree is also referred to as an undergraduate degree to distinguish it from the master's or doctoral degrees, which are graduate degrees. Within the four-year institution, the first two years, freshman and sophomore years, are referred to as lower division. Upper division classes are usually taken by juniors and seniors.

Four-Year Colleges and Universities

College is the general term for a higher education institution, however, there are several levels of 'college' available. The difference between a college and a university technically is the fact that a college offers only bachelor's degrees while a university also offers graduate degrees (master's and doctoral degrees).

Graduate Degrees

The master's degree typically takes about two more years of graduate education after the bachelor's degree and the doctorate or Ph.D. can take another three to six years to complete, depending on the field of study and the institution. A masters degree may require a project or a thesis at the end of the coursework. A thesis is like a short book of original research work completed by the student. The doctoral degree requires that students write a dissertation, a somewhat longer version of the thesis, again based on original research and writing. Both degrees often require that the student pass comprehensive exams covering all their coursework. These comprehensive exams may be oral, written, or both.

Universities differ from each other in the emphasis they place on research as opposed to teaching responsibility for faculty. "Teaching institutions" usually have fewer graduate degree programs and may have no doctoral degrees at all. Faculty at these institutions are expected to teach much more and do somewhat less research and publishing. At "research institutions" there are more doctoral degrees, a greater emphasis on research, publication, and grant writing for faculty, with a somewhat lighter teaching load. The California State University system (CSU), which includes Fresno State among its twenty-two campuses around the state, is an example of a teaching institution. The University of California system (UC), with its nine campuses including Berkeley and UCLA, is an example of a research institution. Both the CSU and the UC systems are public institutions, supported by the state, but there are also many private schools that are teaching or research institutions that are supported by private tuition, large gifts from donors, grant money, and/or religious groups.

The Administration

Faculty are assigned to an academic department. Each department has a chairperson who is also a faculty member in the department and who also teaches classes as part of his or her work load. Departments are organized into bigger groups called either schools or colleges. The head of a school or college (several departments) is called a dean.

The Professor:

Dr. Ruben Sanchez explained his academic background or history at the beginning of his lecture. He teaches in the English Department at California State University, Fresno. A college or university is usually divided into departments by discipline. Each department has a chairman or chairperson who leads the department meetings and represents the department interests to the dean. A dean leads several departments. This grouping of departments has different names at different schools. The grouping may be called a division, a school, or a college. At California State University, Fresno, the organization is as follows:

Dr. Ruben Sanchez - faculty member

⇓

English Department - chairperson

⇓

School of Arts and Humanities - dean

Dr. Sanchez received his bachelor's degree (B.A.) at the University of New Mexico. He got his master's degree (M.A.) and doctoral degree (Ph.D.) from Cornell University, which is in Ithaca, New York.

The Dissertation

Dr. Sanchez said that his dissertation topic was on Milton. The dissertation is the long research paper you must write to complete your doctoral degree. This research paper is usually as long as a book. For a master's degree, a somewhat shorter research paper is usually required, and this paper is called a thesis.

The dissertation topic is usually the area the professor spends a lot of time on later in his or her career. It is the area that he or she specializes in and becomes an expert in. Dr. Sanchez' dissertation topic was Milton. John Milton was an English poet who lived from 1608 to 1674. Dr. Sanchez said that his area of specialization is 17th century literature. The 17th century is 1600 to 1699, and includes writers such as Milton. He also said that he teaches and writes about Shakespeare, the Bible as literature, Chicano literature, and children's literature. The lecture topic he chose to speak to you about was Chicano literature, and specifically, one author, Sandra Cisneros.

ALADIN Dictionary Lesson 2

Table of Contents

1. Thinking   Page 105

2. Person Characteristics   Page 106

3. Importance   Page 109

4. Information   Page 110

5. Research, Academic   Page 111

6. Cause-effect, Change   Page 112

7. Hedge, Qualify   Page 113

8. History, Government, Society   Page 114

9. Time   Page 115

10. Connectors and Comparisons   Page 116

11. Evaluation and Description   Page 117

Alphabetical list of Words/Phrases and Page Numbers in Lesson 2 Dictionary

Word/Phrase	Page	Word/Phrase	Page	Word/Phrase	Page	Word/Phrase	Page
abduct ✂	112	dissertation	111	interpersonal ✂	107	simplistic	108
administrator	114	distinguish from	116	interpretation	105	so-called	114
adolescent	106	dominated by	114	intimate	107	society	115
advocate ✂	112	eloquence ✂	106	limited	113	socioeco-nomic ✂	115
although	116	emergence	112	literally ✂	117	sophisticated ✂	108
ambition	106, 112	empowered ✂	106	literature	111	specialization	112
as early as the 10th century	115	enmeshed in ✂	117	lyrical	117	specter ✂	111
associated with	116	enmity	106	maturity	107	stunning	109
autobiography ✂	111	enthusiasm	106	medium ✔ media = plural	110	subtle	108
awareness (self-awareness)	105	eventful ✂	117	modern civilization	116	symbol	111
baptize ✂	114	explicitly	110	motif	110	symbolically	118
barren	117	extended	116	motivation	107	tenement	115
barrio	114	Far East	114	movement	113	that's all well and good, but	116
basically	113	fellowship ✔	111	mysterious	105	the 19th century	116
Bildungsro-man	111	feminism ✔	105	myth	105	theme	111
blind	105	ferocious	107	narrate	107	therefore	117
but...as well / but also	116	fetter	114	narrative	111	thus	117
by the beginning of the 20th century	115	fiction ✂	110	near and dear	109	universal ✔	109
by the late 1920s	115	first person third person	107	novel ✔ novelist ✂	110	valid	106
central	109	flat ✔	117	omniscient ✂	105, 107	values ✔	106
century ✂	115	formative	112	on behalf of	116	vignette	112
characterize	117	from whence you came	113	oppressive ✂	114	vocation ✂	108
Chicano Chicana	114	fulfill	112	overwhelmed	107	voice ✔	108
Chinese year of the horse	115	gap	117	particularly	118	Western ✔	115
colloquial ✂	117	generalize	110	passage ✔	110	wind up ✔	113
compelling	109	genre	111	patriarchal ✂	115	wisdom	108
conception ✔	105	ghetto	114	per se	116	works ✔	111
conflict	105, 112	golden age	114	perception	105	you might say	114
confusion	105	harsh	117	perhaps	113		
considerable	109	hauntingly ✔	117	perspective ✂	105		
cultural web	110	hero heroine ✂	107	philosophical ✂	107		
cultural myths	110	hint	113	point of view	106		
cultural perspective	110	ideal	117	potential	116		
cultural frames of reference	110	identify with	105, 116	precise	106		
custom	114	identity	107	presumably ✂	113		
decay	112	image	107, 110	process through which	113		
deep ✔	109	immense	109	profound	106, 107		
deserve	109	impact	112	prose	111		
desolate	117	implicit	110	protagonist ✂	108		
despite	116	imply	113	quality ✔	108		
dig more deeply	105	in terms of	116	quarter ✔	115		
disarming ✔✂	106	in a manner of speaking	113	reality	111		
		in the midst of	118	realize	106		
		in 17th century France	116	recipient	113		
		incompre-hensible ✂	107	recruiter	115		
		inevitable	112	relevant	109		
		influence	113	relies on	116		
		inherit	113	reputation	108		
		initial ✔	116	role ✔	108		
		inner city	114	roots ✔	108		
				seems to	113		
				sentimental	108		
				significance	109		

1. Thinking

Noun	Verb	Adjective	Adverb	Definition	Example
awareness (self-awareness)		aware		n. understanding, learning, seeing	She went from confusion to **awareness**.
blindness	**blind**	blind	blindly	v. stop from seeing or understanding	Our culture selectively **blinds** us.
conception ✔ concept	conceive of	conceivable	conceivably	n. idea, understanding	Esperanza developed a **conception** of her ideal house.
conflict	conflict			n. disagreement, argument, struggle	The **conflict** in the book is Esperanza's attempt to understand who she is.
confusion	confuse	confused	confusedly	n. no understanding, poor thinking	She went from an initial state of **confusion** to awareness.
	dig more deeply ✔			v. try to understand better by thinking more about it	We need to **dig more deeply** into the text to understand what the text is really about.
feminism ✔ feminist				n. belief in equal rights for women	**Feminism** is a perspective or belief system.
identity identification	**identify with**			v. see yourself as similar to something	Esperanza **identified with** the four skinny trees.
interpretation interpreter	interpret	interpretable		n. way of understanding	Novels were a medium for the **interpretation** of life.
mystery		**mysterious**	mysteriously	adj. not easy to understand, unknown	The three **mysterious** old ladies gave Esperanza a wish.
myth mythology		mythical	mythically	n. traditional story, legend	We share certain cultural **myths**.
omniscience		**omniscient** ✂	omnisciently	adj. knowing everything	A third person narrator provides the **omniscient** point of view.
perception	perceive	perceptive	perceptively	n. idea, image, thought, understanding	Esperanza developed a **perception** of herself as a writer.
perspective ✂				n. point of view, the way you think about something, opinion	Feminism is a **perspective** or point of view.

Noun	Verb	Adjective	Adverb	Definition	Example
point of view				n. the way you think, your opinion	She writes from the **point of view** of her culture.
precision		**precise**	precisely	adj. exact, correct, accurate	We will learn some terms so we have a more **precise** vocabulary for discussing this book.
profundity		**profound**	profoundly	adj. deep, more than just what you see on the surface, complex	It is a very **profound** text.
realization	**realize**			v. understand fully, learn	She **realized** she would always return to Mango Street.
validity validation	validate	**valid**	validly	adj. true, correct, based on true information	She has written something **valid** and relevant.
values ✔	value	valued		n. standards, what people think is right or wrong	We share certain customs and **values**.

2. Person Characteristics

Noun	Verb	Adjective	Adverb	Definition	Example
adolescent adolescence		**adolescent**		n. the time when you are young, about age 12-17, not quite mature	Authors attempt to generalize about their own **adolescent** experiences.
ambition		ambitious	ambitiously	n. what you want to do or be in the future	Her great grandmother could not fulfill her goals or ambitions.
disarmament	disarm	**disarming** ✔ ✂	disarmingly	adj. seeming to be friendly, simple, not suspicious or dangerous	One of the **disarming** qualities of the writing is the simple language the author used.
eloquence ✂		eloquent	eloquently	n. beautiful writing, words, speaking	The vignettes are stunning for their **eloquence**.
empowerment	empower	**empowered** ✂ **self-empowered**		adj. given power, getting power over oneself	Esperanza will break free and return **empowered** as a writer.
enmity				n. hostility, active hatred	She faced the specter of racial **enmity**.
enthusiasm	enthuse	enthusiastic	enthusiastically	n. great interest, positive support, excitement	There's lots of **enthusiasm** about Cisneros.

Noun	Verb	Adjective	Adverb	Definition	Example
ferocity		**ferocious**	ferociously	adj. fierce, scary, aggressive	The trees send **ferocious** roots beneath the ground.
first person third person				n. person refers to the pronouns and point of view used; first person is I, we; third person uses he, she, it, they	The story is narrated in the **first person**. The **third person** is the omniscient point of view.
hero heroine ✄		heroic		n. a man or woman who is very brave, or the main character in a story	The protagonist is the **hero** or **heroine** of the story.
identity	identify			n. how a person thinks about himself or herself, who they think they are like	Mango Street is part of her **identity**.
image imagery				n. mental or imaginary picture	She presents this **image** of her great grandmother sitting by the window.
incompre-hension		**incompre-hensible** ✄	incomprehensibly	adj. can not be understood, completely unclear	The text appears **incomprehensible**.
		interpersonal ✄		adj. speaking, activity between persons	They wrote about complex **interpersonal** relations.
intimacy		**intimate**	intimately	adj. warm, informal, friendly, personal	The first person point of view is more **intimate** and personal.
maturity maturation	mature	mature	maturely	n. reaching adult age	It is a story about a young person who is moving from childhood to **maturity**.
motivation motive	motivate	motivated		n. the reason you do something	They wrote about relations and **motivations**.
narrator narration narrative	**narrate**	narrative		v. to tell the story	This story is **narrated** in the first person.
omniscience		**omniscient** ✄	omnisciently	adj. having all understanding, universal understanding, knowing everything	Third person is the **omniscient** or God-like point of view.
	overwhelm	**overwhelmed** overwhelming	overwhelmingly	adj. taken over, covered over, feeling like something is too big to handle	Esperanza had a desire not to be **overwhelmed** like her great grandmother was.
philosophy	philosophize	**philosophical** ✄	philosophically	n. relating to deep thinking about something	The novel replaced religious and **philosophical** works.
profundity		**profound**	profoundly	adj. deep thinking, important ideas	It is a very deep and **profound** book.

Noun	Verb	Adjective	Adverb	Definition	Example
protagonist ✂				n. the main character in a story	The **protagonist** is the central character.
quality ✔				n. characteristic, nature, tone	The book has a disarming **quality**.
reputation	repute	reputable reputed	reputably	n. the knowledge people have about you, what people know, say, and think about you.	Her **reputation** is growing and she is becoming better known throughout the country.
role ✔				n. what you do in your life, or the part played by an actor	Her great grandmother played the traditional female **role**.
roots ✔				n. your family background, ancestors	She would always return to Mango Street and her cultural perspective or **roots**.
sentiment sentimentality	sentimentalize	**sentimental**	sentimentally	adj. with strong feelings, emotional rather than factual	The novels became more **sentimental**.
simplification	simplify	**simplistic**	simplistically	adj. very simple in a negative way, not complex or sophisticated	It may appear to be a simplistic text.
sophistication		**sophisticated** ✂	sophisticatedly	adj. high level, complex, not simple, educated	A formal tone is more **sophisticated**, more grammatically correct.
subtlety		**subtle**	subtly	adj. not direct, not obvious, understated, low-key	The novelist was **subtle** in her use of symbols.
vocation ✂		vocational		n. job, profession, occupation	Esperanza will use her **vocation** as a writer to remember from whence she came.
voice ✔				n. the way somebody talks, not the sound of the voice itself	The author used an informal tone of **voice**.
wisdom		wise	wisely	n. knowledge, good judgment that you get with time as you grow up	The main character learns **wisdom** the hard way.

3. Importance

Noun	Verb	Adjective	Adverb	Definition	Example
centrality		**central**	centrally	adj. main, important	The **central** character is a young girl.
	compel	**compelling**	compellingly	adj. causes you to think or do something	The book is intensely **compelling**.
		considerable	considerably	adj. much, very much, a lot	The novel had **considerable** impact on the feminist community.
depth		**deep** ✔	deeply	adj. with important thoughts, information, not simple	It is a **deep** and profound story.
	deserve	deserving		v. it should get something, people should think about it, it is important	The book **deserves** serious literary consideration.
immensity		**immense**	immensely	n. very very large	France produced an **immense** number of novels.
		near and dear		adj. important, near you and dear (special) to you or important to you, close	Esperanza's experiences are **near and dear** to the author's.
relevance		**relevant**	relevantly	adj. important, related to the topic	Cisneros has something valid and **relevant** to say.
significance		significant	significantly	n. importance	We want to understand the **significance** of wanting to leave and needing to come back.
	stun	**stunning**	stunningly	adj. surprising, very beautiful, very noticeable, unusual	Her writing is **stunning** for its eloquence.
universe universality		**universal** ✔	universally	adj. seen everywhere, known by everyone	The author made her experiences a **universal** symbol of adolescence.

4. Information

Noun	Verb	Adjective	Adverb	Definition	Example
cultural frames of reference				n. frame of references is the way we think, the context, the information we use to understand something	Our ways of thinking are related to our **cultural frames of reference**.
cultural myths				n. the beliefs of a certain culture, not necessarily facts	We share certain **cultural myths**.
cultural web				n. the knowledge and symbols of our culture that stay around us, are part of us	We live enmeshed in this **cultural web**.
cultural perspective				n. point of view, thoughts that show her culture, her background	Cisneros writes from her own **cultural perspective**.
explicitness		explicit	**explicitly**	adv. obviously, straight forward, not implicit or implied	The work is **explicitly** feminist.
fiction ✀	fictionalize	fictional	fictionally	n. writing that is imagination, not true, a story that is made up	Cisneros writes **fiction**.
generality generalization generalizability	**generalize**	generalizable generalized		v. use the same knowledge or information in all situations, all the time	Autobiographical novels attempt to **generalize** the author's own experiences to others.
image		imaginary		n. a picture in your mind, mental idea or picture	She presents the **image** of her great grandmother sitting by the window.
		implicit	implicitly	adj. internal, inside, not clearly stated, implied	There are **implicit** motifs of struggle and success.
medium ✔ media = plural				n. a way of passing information to the public	The novel is giving way to the **medium** of film.
motif				n. theme, main idea	There are implicit **motifs** of struggle, conflict, and success.
novel ✔ novelist ✀		novelistic		n. fiction, story, not factual writing	Bildungsroman is a **novel** of growing up or formation.
passage ✔				n. a short piece of writing	The short **passages** are vignettes.

110

Noun	Verb	Adjective	Adverb	Definition	Example
reality		real		n. the things and events that are real, not imaginary, not always the way we want them to be, but the way they are	She discovers the hard **realities** of life.
specter ✂				n. ghost, something that haunts us, bothers us	She faced the **specter** of racial enmity.
symbol	symbolize	symbolic	symbolically	n. some thing or picture that represents or stands for another thing	For Esperanza, her house, her place, is a **symbol** for her identity.
theme		thematic	thematically	n. main story, main idea	They develop this **theme** of growing up and education.
works ✔				n. the writing, art, or music that someone produces, all their work	The novel replaced religious and scientific **works** for many readers.

5. Research, Academic

Noun	Verb	Adjective	Adverb	Definition	Example
autobiography ✂		autobiographical	autobiographically	n. writing the story of your own life	Mango Street is fiction, so it is not really **autobiography**.
Bildungsroman				n. a story of growing up and learning about life	**Bildungsroman** is a German word meaning novel of educational formation.
dissertation				n. the long piece of research and writing you do to complete a doctoral degree (Ph.D.)	I wrote my **dissertation** on Milton.
fellowship ✔				n. the money you get to study or to do some work, like a scholarship	Cisneros was the recipient of two NEA **fellowships**.
genre				n. a kind of writing, music or art, a particular style	The **genre** of the Western novel has a long history.
literature		literary literate		n. the writing of a particular culture or country	Dr. Sanchez teaches Chicano **literature.**
narration **narrator**	narrate	**narrative**		adj. telling a story	The novel is a **narrative** art form.
prose				n. writing that is similar to everyday speech, not poetry	Extended **prose** works began in 17th century France.

Noun	Verb	Adjective	Adverb	Definition	Example
specialization	specialize	special	specially	n. the area you know the most about, the area you are an expert in	My area of **specialization** is 17th century literature.
vignette				n. a French word that means s short descriptive piece of writing	The series of **vignettes** are short chapters.

6. Cause-Effect, Change

Noun	Verb	Adjective	Adverb	Definition	Example
abduction	**abduct** ✀			v. kidnapped, stolen	Her great grandmother was **abducted** by her great grandfather.
advocate advocacy	**advocate** ✀			v. fight for, argue for, push for	Feminism **advocates** political equality.
ambition		ambitious	ambitiously	n. your goals in life, what you want	Her great grandmother was prevented from fulfilling any kind of goals or **ambitions**.
conflict		conflicting		n. problem, disagreement, argument, war, struggle	There has to be some kind of **conflict** to begin with and then some kind of understanding.
decay	decay	decayed decaying		n. decline, die out, fall apart, rot, become unhealthy	The novel has shown signs of **decay** as an art form.
emergence	emerge	emerging		n. coming out, appearance, recognition	Mango Street signals the **emergence** of a major new author.
formation	form	**formative**	formatively	adj. time of change, formation, growing up years	The novels deal with the **formative** years.
			from whence you came	adv. where you came from, a poetic way of saying where you are from	Coming back means remembering **from whence you came**.
fulfillment	**fulfill**	fulfilled fulfilling		n. being satisfied, reaching your goals or dreams	Her great grandmother was prevented from **fulfilling** any kind of goals or ambitions.
impact	impact			n. influence, cause for change, effect	The novel has had considerable **impact** on the feminist community.

Noun	Verb	Adjective	Adverb	Definition	Example
inevitability		**inevitable**	inevitably	adj. something that is expected to happen, no surprise, happens eventually	The story of adolescence has an **inevitable** appeal for the novelist.
influence	influence	influential	influentially	n. causes change, affects	The cultural web **influences** the way we think.
inheritance	**inherit**	inherited		v. to get from your family, usually after someone dies	Esperanza **inherited** her great grandmother's name.
movement	move			n. change, progress	The Bildungsroman concerns some kind of **movement** from confusion to awareness.
process through which				n. how something happens	The book is about the **process through which** the young girl reaches self-awareness.
recipient	receive			n. the person who receives or gets something	She was the **recipient** of two NEA fellowships.
	wind up ✔			v. end up, come to in the end	Esperanza will **wind up** returning to Mango Street, at least in her writing.

7. Hedge, Qualify

Hedge Word or Phrase	Explanation	Example
basically	not completely the same, mostly the same	A chapter and a vignette are basically the same thing.
hint	small piece of information that makes you think about the similarity between Esperanza and the trees	The trees grow despite the concrete and that's a hint about Esperanza's situation.
imply	a circle suggests return - it does not necessarily mean return	A circle implies that she will have to return to her past.
in a manner of speaking	sort of, something like a children's story - not completely	In a manner of speaking, it is a children's story.
limited	not full, not the maximum	The first person is a limited point of view.
perhaps	we don't know for sure, but it is possible to believe that this is true	You can perhaps assume that Esperanza's experiences are like those of the author.
presumably ✂	we believe this can happen in the future and that it will probably happen, but we are not sure	She will presumably be able to return to her past by writing about it.

seems to	may have, probably have - the speaker is not sure		The novel seems to have its beginnings in Goethe's works.
so-called	people call it a chapter but it is not really a chapter		This so-called chapter is actually a vignette.
you might say	some people believe this - the author is stating it this way to indicate that not all people would agree with this		The idea of place is part of the theme, you might say.

8. History, Government, Society

Noun	Verb	Adjective	Adverb	Definition	Example
administrator	administer	administrative	administratively	n. the person who directs or leads an organization	She was an arts administrator.
baptism	**baptize** ✂	baptized baptismal		v. a Christian tradition at which time a baby is given his name and brought into the church community	Esperanza said, "I would like to **baptize** myself under a new name."
barrio				n. Spanish word meaning an area or district of a city, usually a poor area	She grew up in the Hispanic **barrio** or ghetto.
Chicano Chicana		**Chicano Chicana**		n. an American of Mexican descent	I teach the Bible and **Chicano** literature.
custom		customary	customarily	n. what people usually do, habits, traditions	People have a shared set of **customs** and values.
domination	dominate	**dominated by**		adj. controlled by	A patriarchal society is **dominated** by males.
Far East				n. countries of East Asia including China, Japan, Korea, and sometimes including Southeast Asia	In the **Far East**, novels began a separate development.
fetter				n. literally a chain on the feet, figuratively something that holds you back	She discovers the hard realities of life, the **fetters** of class and gender.
ghetto				n. the area of a city where one kind of people live who are restricted there for economic reasons or social discrimination	She grew up in the Hispanic barrio or **ghetto**.
golden age				n. the best time, the ideal time, the most popular time	The 19th century was the **golden age** of the novel.
inner city				n. near the center of a city, often the old, poor part of the city, not suburbs	She lives in the **inner city** or barrio.

Noun	Verb	Adjective	Adverb	Definition	Example
oppression	oppress	**oppressive** ✂	oppressively	adj. pushing somebody down, controlling with power	She wanted a place of her own in the midst of her **oppressive** surroundings.
patriarchy		**patriarchal** ✂		adj. a society or family in which the male or father is the leader	A **patriarchal** society is dominated by males.
quarter ✔				n. a certain part of the city, a certain district or area	She grew up in the Hispanic **quarter** of Chicago.
recruiter recruit	recruit			n. the person who tries to get other people to participate or join	Cisneros was a college **recruiter**.
		socioeconomic ✂		adj. describes a person's social and economic status or background	She has a harsh **socioeconomic** background.
society		societal		n. the culture we live in, the people we live with in our country	A patriarchal **society** is dominated by males.
tenement				n. slum, poor area of town with bad housing	She wanted to escape the run-down tenements.
		Western ✔		adj. the countries and cultures in the Western Hemisphere and Europe; not Asian, not African	The **Western** novel is a product of modern civilization.

9. Time

Noun	Verb	Adjective	Adverb	Definition	Example
as early as the 10th century				n. the years 900-999	In the Far East, novels began **as early as the 10th century**.
by the late 1920s				n. about 1927-1929	**By the late 1920s** the novel had begun to show signs of decay.
by the beginning of the 20th century				n. the 20th century began in the year 1900; this is the 20th century right now	**By the beginning of the 20th century** the novel had become the most common form of reading matter.
century ✂				n. 100 years; counting centuries began with zero, so 0-99 was the first century. We are now in the 20th century-1900-1999	The 19th **century** was the golden age of the novel.

Noun	Verb	Adjective	Adverb	Definition	Example
Chinese year of the horse				n. Each year in the Chinese calendar is associated with one of 12 animals. The year in which you were born is believed to have given you some characteristics of that animal.	She was born like me in the **Chinese year of the horse**.
extension	extend	**extended** extensive	extensively	adj. longer than usual, long	**Extended** prose works became popular.
in 17th century France				n. the years 1600-1699	Extended prose works began **in 17th century France**.
initiation	initiate initialize	**initial** ✔	initially	adj. beginning, first	The main character moves from some sort of **initial** confusion to understanding.
modern civilization				n. refers to a time period after the Middle Ages, from about 1450 to the present	The western novel is a product of **modern civilization**.
potential		**potential**	potentially	adj. something that can happen in the future	The writer must assess the **potential** audience.
the 19th century				n. the years 1800-1899	**The 19th century** was the golden age of the novel.

10. Connectors and Comparisons

Connector	Meaning and use	Example
although	even though, in spite of the fact that	Although she wanted to leave, she knew she would always return.
associated with	connected to, related to, part of	There is a kind of sadness that is somehow associated with her name.
but...as well / but also	also, in addition	It means sadness but it means hope as well. It means sadness but it also means hope.
despite	in spite of, anyhow, even though	She said that the trees grow despite the concrete.
distinguish from	see a difference between two things	You must distinguish the author from the character in the book.
identify with	see yourself like another person, understand the other person	She identifies with her great grandmother who was also named Esperanza. Esperanza identifies with the trees.
in terms of	using thse words, using that idea	It is difficult to talk about these divisions in terms of chapters because they are so short.
on behalf of	for someone, to help someone	Feminists advocate on behalf of women's rights.
per se	Latin - by itself, in itself, only. Not just the Mango Street house - the ideal house	We want to understand what a house means to Esperanza, not the House on Mango Street per se, but the ideal house.

Connector	Meaning and use	Example
relies on	uses the method, needs, counts on	The writer relies on your stored knowledge.
that's all well and good, but	it's OK, but it is not enough; something else is needed, necessary	That's all well and good that she wants to escape, but she must learn she has to come back.
therefore	thus, as a result, for that reason - signals reaching a conclusion about something	Feminism advocates equality and therefore is organized around activity on behalf of women's rights.
thus	therefore, as a result, because of - signals reaching a conclusion about something	Thus although Esperanza wanted a house of her own, she knew she would always return to Mango Street.

11. Evaluation and Description

Noun	Verb	Adjective	Adverb	Definition	Example
barrenness		**barren**		adj. not producing much, empty	This may be a temporarily **barren** period for the novel.
character characteristic	**characterize**	characteristic	characteristically	v. have the qualities of, be like, be described as	Our beliefs might be **characterized** as cultural myths.
colloquialism		**colloquial** ✄	colloquially	adj. conversational, not formal language, not academic language	It makes use of **colloquial** language instead of very formal language.
desolation		**desolate**	desolately	adj. lonely, ugly, without anything pretty or nice	Mango Street is a **desolate** landscape.
	enmesh	**enmeshed in** ✄		adj. tangled, caught in a mesh or net	We live **enmeshed** in this cultural web.
event		**eventful** ✄	eventfully	adj. happening often, frequently happening, many things happening	Novels became more popular and **eventful**.
flat ✔				n. a kind of apartment	Not a **flat**. Not an apartment in back.
gap				n. empty space, missing information	The author relies on your knowledge to fill in the **gaps** left vacant in the text.
	haunt	haunting	**hauntingly** ✔	adv. not easily forgotten, always remembered again and again, strange	Mango Street is **hauntingly** lyrical.
harshness		**harsh**	harshly	adj. rough, severe, very difficult	She comes from a socioeconomic background that is particularly **harsh** on her.
ideal	idealize	**ideal**	ideally	adj. the best possible	Esperanza thinks about the **ideal** house for her.
literalness		literal	**literally** ✄	adv. actually, really, not figuratively or symbolically	She won't **literally** escape Mango Street, but she will escape symbolically.

117

Noun	Verb	Adjective	Adverb	Definition	Example
lyric, lyricism, lyricist		**lyrical**	lyrically	adj. lyrics are the words to a song; lyrical writing is therefore beautiful writing	Mango street is hauntingly **lyrical**.
		in the midst of		adj. in the middle of	She wanted space **in the midst** of her oppressive surroundings.
		particular	**particularly**	adv. very, especially	Her socioeconomic background is **particularly** harsh.
symbol	symbolize	symbolic	**symbolically**	adv. not really, not literally; figuratively, not actually	She won't literally escape Mango Street, but she will escape **symbolically**.

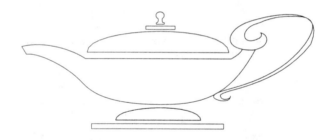

*A*cademic *L*anguage: *A*ssessment and *D*evelopment of *I*ndividual *N*eeds

ALADIN

Lesson 3

ALADIN Lesson 3   Table of Contents

Table of Contents   120

Self-Assessments of Lesson 3 Vocabulary   121

1. Note-taking - Lecture has three segments of about 10 minutes

    A. Lecture Note-taking   123
    Lecture Part A Note-taking   124
    Lecture Question Part A   125
    Lecture Part B Note-taking   126
    Lecture Question Part B   127
    Lecture Part C Note-taking   128
    Lecture Question Part C   129
    Lecture Signals and Note-taking Skills   130
    Lawyers, Argument, and Debate   132

    B. Reading Note-taking   133
    Reading - Part 1   134
    Reading Notes and Summary - Part 1   135
    Reading - Part 2   136
    Reading Notes and Summary - Part 2   137

2. Academic Vocabulary Building   138
    Latin Words and Phrases   141
    Word Forms and Vocabulary Practice   143

3. Reading Skills and Strategies   148
    Reading Practice - Supreme Court   149

4. Sentence Complexity: Connectors   150

5. Academic Culture   151
    Law School and Academic Legal Issues   151

Dictionary Lesson 3   153

Lesson 3 VOCABULARY SELF-ASSESSMENT - READING

DIRECTIONS: Circle the number that shows how well you know each word below.	**1** I don't recognize this word.	**2** I've **seen** this word before but I don't know what it means.	**3** I **think** I know what this word means but I am not 100% sure.	**4** I know what this word means and I can **probably** use it in a sentence.	**5** I know this word and I have used it recently in speaking or writing.
1. prior	1	2	3	4	5
2. synonymous	1	2	3	4	5
3. tribunal	1	2	3	4	5
4. federal	1	2	3	4	5
5. per se	1	2	3	4	5
6. deem	1	2	3	4	5
7. discretion	1	2	3	4	5
8. initiate	1	2	3	4	5
9. oath	1	2	3	4	5
10. testimony	1	2	3	4	5
11. credibility	1	2	3	4	5
12. authorize	1	2	3	4	5
13. indict	1	2	3	4	5
14. preponderance	1	2	3	4	5
15. circumstance	1	2	3	4	5
16. inadequate	1	2	3	4	5
17. unanimous	1	2	3	4	5
18. civil	1	2	3	4	5
19. liable	1	2	3	4	5
20. negligent	1	2	3	4	5
21. spouse	1	2	3	4	5
22. hypothetical	1	2	3	4	5
23. allege	1	2	3	4	5
24. credibility	1	2	3	4	5
25. transcript	1	2	3	4	5

Lesson 3 VOCABULARY SELF-ASSESSMENT - DICTATION

DIRECTIONS: Circle the number that shows how well you know each word you write below.	**1** I don't recognize this word.	**2** I've **seen** this word before but I don't know what it means.	**3** I **think** I know what this word means but I am not 100% sure.	**4** I know what this word means and I can **probably** use it in a sentence.	**5** I know this word and I have used it recently in speaking or writing.
1.	1	2	3	4	5
2.	1	2	3	4	5
3.	1	2	3	4	5
4.	1	2	3	4	5
5.	1	2	3	4	5
6.	1	2	3	4	5
7.	1	2	3	4	5
8.	1	2	3	4	5
9.	1	2	3	4	5
10.	1	2	3	4	5
11.	1	2	3	4	5
12.	1	2	3	4	5
13.	1	2	3	4	5
14.	1	2	3	4	5
15.	1	2	3	4	5
16.	1	2	3	4	5
17.	1	2	3	4	5
18.	1	2	3	4	5
19.	1	2	3	4	5
20.	1	2	3	4	5
21.	1	2	3	4	5
22.	1	2	3	4	5
23.	1	2	3	4	5
24.	1	2	3	4	5
25.	1	2	3	4	5

READ ME

1. Note-taking

This lesson begins with an academic vocabulary self-assessment. At the end of this lesson you may do this assessment again. Self-assessment is a very good way to find out what you know and how well you know it. There is no grade on this assessment. It is just used to help you and your instructor know what your starting knowledge level is on some of the academic vocabulary.

In Lesson 3 you will listen to a lecture by Dr. Ida Jones, a professor in the School of Business Administration. She is a lawyer and her lecture is about the legal system. The lecture is divided into three ten-minute segments. You will be taking notes on each segment.

Each lecture section also has a question you will answer using your lecture notes. After you answer the questions, the instructor will show you model notes and model answers for the questions.

In the second part of the lesson, you will be underlining and taking notes from some academic reading about the legal system. You will also be writing summaries of the reading. Your instructor will show you model reading notes and model summaries.

The rest of the lesson, like Lessons 1 and 2, includes reading strategies, academic vocabulary building, practice with long sentences, and academic culture. Because lawyers have to have good speaking skills to make their arguments in court, in this lesson you will also get some practice with your speaking skills using academic language. Your teacher will set up debate teams in class and you will have a debate tournament!

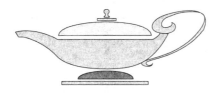

Lesson 3 LECTURE NOTES   Part A

Use the following two pages to take notes from Part A of the lecture. This section is about 10 minutes long. The information in your notes will be used to answer a question later.

_____

_____

_____

_____

_____

_____

_____

_____

_____

_____

_____

_____

_____

_____

_____

_____

_____

_____

_____

_____

_____

_____

Continue Taking Notes on Next Page

_____

_____

_____

_____

_____

_____

_____

_____

_____

_____

_____

_____

_____

_____

Lecture Question Part A. Use your lecture notes from **Part A** to answer the following question. Use complete sentences.

Explain the difference between how civil and criminal court cases are started. In other words, who starts the lawsuit?

_____

_____

_____

_____

_____

_____

_____

_____

_____

_____

Lesson 3 LECTURE NOTES Part B

Use the following two pages to take notes from Part B of the lecture. This section is about 10 minutes long. The information in your notes will be used to answer a question later.

_____

_____

_____

_____

_____

_____

_____

_____

_____

_____

_____

_____

_____

_____

_____

_____

_____

_____

_____

_____

_____

_____

_____

_____

_____

Continue Taking Notes on Next Page

_____

_____

_____

_____

_____

_____

_____

_____

_____

_____

_____

Lecture Question Part B. Use your lecture notes from **Part B** to answer the following question. Use complete sentences.

Explain when the court needs to use *in rem jurisdiction*.

_____

_____

_____

_____

_____

_____

_____

_____

_____

_____

_____

_____

Lesson 3 LECTURE NOTES Part C

Use the following two pages to take notes from Part C of the lecture. This section is about 10 minutes long. The information in your notes will be used to answer a question later.

_____

_____

_____

_____

_____

_____

_____

_____

_____

_____

_____

_____

_____

_____

_____

_____

_____

_____

_____

_____

_____

_____

_____

Continue Taking Notes on Next Page

Part C Continued

_____

_____

_____

_____

_____

_____

_____

_____

_____

_____

Lecture Question Part C. Use your lecture notes from **Part C** to answer the following question. Use complete sentences.

List five kinds of cases that are heard in Superior Court.

_____

_____

_____

_____

_____

_____

_____

_____

_____

_____

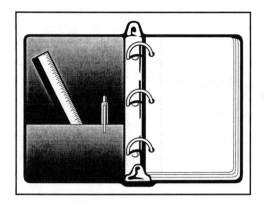

Lecture Signals -

Dr. Ida Jones

We saw in Lesson 1 that lectures have a structure or organization. The professor gives you signals about what is important to write down. When you are reading, these signals about what is important are indicated by titles, subtitles, paragraph breaks, bolding, and also by some of the same signals professors use when they speak. In lectures, you can't see the signals like you can in reading. Since professors speak so quickly and so much during a college course, you need to practice listening for the signals about what is important to write down. In Lesson 1 we organized lecture signals into the following categories:

Lecture Signals

Signal Category	Explanation	Example
I. Topic Marker	tells you what the topic is	Today's lecture is on... The next issue we will discuss is...
II. Checkpoint Marker	tells you where the professor is in a lecture or when the professor is changing to a new topic or concluding the lecture	
A. Topic Shifter	may be an aside - almost spoken to himself/herself at the end of a particular point	Now... OK.... Let's see... Right... Alright...
B. Concluder	signals end of topic or end of lecture	That's what you need to know about... That covers the topic of...
III. Information Expander	these are important signals that give the following kinds of information:	
A. Give background information	gives the historical or social context	As you may remember from history... During this time period we also saw...
B. Explain meaning	gives a definition or restatement of the topic or idea	In other words... By this I mean...
C. Give an example	could also be anecdote (little personal story) or joke	For example... In the real world this would be... In terms of...
D. Relate two pieces of information:	often uses "Connector" words and phrases (see vocabulary section)	
1. Cause-effect	how "A" causes "B" to happen	The result of this is... This causes the following to happen...

2. Contrast	how are "A" and "B" different	In contrast... On the other hand... The opposite is true for...
3. Compare	how are "A" and "B" the same	All three men believe... Similarly...
IV. Information Qualifier	gives a different value to the information	
A. Emphasize importance of information	draws your attention to the important points in the lecture	repetition, restatement
1. Rhetorical question*	a question asked of the whole class - no answer is expected	What do you think he did next? What do you think the answer is?
2. Imperative*	an "order" to the students	Remember this. Write this down.
3. Direct statement of importance	the professor tells you directly how important something is	This is important. Pay particular attention to this point.
B. Information Corrector	professor made a mistake and his correcting himself/herself	Oh, what I meant to say was...
C. Emphasize information is not very important	extra information you don't have to write down - added to make the lecture more interesting	This may not be relevant but... By the way...
V. Summarizer	professor will summarize or restate the important information	In summary...As I said before... In other words...

* rhetorical question - When someone asks a rhetorical question, he or she expects no answer. It is just a question that guides the lecture or conversation. For example, when you are driving, you may ask about a driver in front of you, "What is that crazy guy doing?" You really don't expect anyone in the car to answer this rhetorical question.

* imperative sentence - This kind of sentence is like an order. You are telling someone what to do. The sentence usually starts with a verb: Bring me the book. Open the window. The professor is telling you to focus your attention on something: Consider the following.

Practice 1

➡ **TASK:**   Read the following signals that Dr. Jones gave you during the lecture. Decide the type of lecture signal and the meaning in small groups or with the whole class.

Dr. Jones said:	Lecture Signal:	Meaning:
1. I am going to focus on the municipal courts.		
2. Now how do you tell what is a misdemeanor case?		

3. In the law we like to use Latin terms so you have to hire us to figure out what they mean.		
4. A civil case is .... A criminal case is different.		
5. We will dissect the court procedure by starting with a sample case.		
6. Specifically what we are going to be looking at is how individuals get cases into court.		
7. Now a summons is just a piece of paper that basically says you have been sued.		

Lawyers, Argument, and Debate

A good way to learn academic language is to practice using the words and phrases you are learning when you speak. In order to improve your language and speaking skills, your class will have some debates on topics of interest.

When lawyers present their cases in court, they have to speak well and persuasively in order to convince the judge and jury that their client is innocent or that the other party is guilty. Lawyers don't often argue with each other; they are usually arguing in a way to convince the judge and the jury of a particular opinion. Politicians also speak this way when they make speeches or when they debate other politicians before an election.

In high school and college, you can join a club in order to learn how to make good arguments. Your school may have a debate team that travels to other schools and tournaments in order to have debate competitions. There are state and national debate champions, just like in other sports, for both high school and college teams. There are many forms of debate and public speaking competitions. They all are under the broad category called *forensics*. Forensics comes from a Latin word that means public. So, forensics includes arguments or exercises suitable for the public courts or public discussion. You may have heard of forensic medicine, which has to do with relating medical facts to legal problems.

There are some general rules to follow when you prepare for your debate.

1. You will not be arguing directly with the other team. Like a lawyer, you will be trying to persuade a judge or judges about how good and logical your argument is and your facts are, and why your argument is better than the other team's argument.

2. Debate teams must prepare to argue both sides of a case. By reading about and understanding both sides of the argument, a debate team can be prepared to argue against the other side. Before the debate, the decision is made with a flip of a coin which team has the

affirmative (agree) and which team has the negative (disagree) position.

3. The issue to be debated is stated as a resolution. For example, "Resolved: Animals should be used in medical research." The Affirmative team then argues in favor or in support of this resolution. The Negative team argues against it.

4. Time limits are strictly enforced. Usually each team gets 8 minutes to state their argument, 5 minutes rebuttal of the other team's argument, and 3 minutes to cross examine the other team.

Rebuttal means arguing against the other team's argument - stating what is wrong with their argument. Cross examination means asking about the sources of information that support the argument. In other words, you can't just make up information. If you state a fact, you have to have a reference for that fact. During cross examination you can also ask the other team about the logic of their argument or their ideas. For example, they may have facts or evidence that seem to contradict other evidence they presented.

Your team can take notes while the other team is talking -- this is called 'flowing' the argument and the notes you take are called a 'flow'.

5. You can't interrupt the other team while they are talking. You also can't be impolite, but you can be forceful and aggressive in your argument.

6. Usually individual students get speaker points during the debate from the judges. If your judges give individual points, the points can be used to give special awards to individual students. Or your judges may give points to the whole team instead of to individuals on the team. The team with the most points wins the debate. Points are given in six categories, with a maximum of 5 points per category (30 points total possible):

1. Clarity (how clear your arguments are)
2. Organization (how organized the team is)
3. Evidence (facts you collected)
4. Argumentation (organization of argument and preparation)
5. Presentation (how well you present your argument)
6. Courtesy (how polite you are to the other team)

Your teacher will pass out score cards for the judges during your debates.

6. You should probably give different speaking jobs to different team members. One can specialize in the affirmative case, another in the negative. A third member can prepare the cross examination, and the fourth member can do the rebuttal. All members can work on taking notes (the flow) while the other team is speaking.

B. Reading Note-taking and Summarizing.
Remember to use the Pre-Reading and During-Reading Strategies you learned in Lesson 2!

Pre-Reading: What is this about? What kinds of information will I be seeing?

During-Reading: How well did I understand this sentence? Can I guess at any new vocabulary? Can I break this sentence into smaller pieces? Is this important? Should I underline part or all of this sentence?

READING PART 1: *Underline the important information on the page, including the information in the box.*

The Function of Courts

The word "court" has various meanings. At times it is synonymous with "judge," as when a judge tells an attorney to address his or her remarks "to the court and not to the opposing counsel." At other times it indicates the place where a trial takes place. Usually, however, court means a tribunal established by the state or federal government for the administration of justice.

The main function of a court is to decide controversies between parties in a lawsuit, called the litigation, which comes to us from a Latin root meaning *to dispute*. The parties in dispute are called litigants, and the court's decision is called a judgment. Since the court's main function is to resolve disputes, it ordinarily will not answer hypothetical questions; it will not advise, for example, what a person's rights would be under a proposed contract. Besides the judge, a court also has a bailiff which is a person who keeps order in the court.

Procedures Prior to Trial

Complaint

The party who initiates a civil lawsuit is called the plaintiff. The party being sued is called the defendant. The plaintiff initiates a lawsuit by filing with the court a statement variously called a complaint, petition, or declaration. The complaint must contain a statement of the facts constituting the cause of action, in ordinary and concise language, and a demand of the relief which the plaintiff claims. For example, the plaintiff may state, "On January 1, the defendant drove his automobile in a negligent manner and collided with the plaintiff, causing great bodily injury." The plaintiff would then request damages in a certain amount, such as $100,000.

Depositions

A deposition is a statement under oath made at a hearing held out of court before the trial. The purposes of depositions are for the lawyers on each side to discover what the testimony will be at the trial, to obtain this testimony while it is still fresh in the minds of the witnesses, and to preserve the testimony in case the witness is not available during the trial. A court reporter records the questions and answers and prepares a written transcript for the witness to sign. In recent years, many courts have encouraged the use of videotaped depositions. These videotapes can be viewed during the trial and the judge and jury can view the witness and better evaluate the person's credibility.

Reading Notes Part 1. Use the space below to take notes from the section of the text that is enclosed in a box. The information in your notes will be used to answer a question later.

_____

_____

_____

_____

_____

_____

_____

_____

_____

_____

Reading Summary Part 1:

Write a summary of the section in the box. Use your own words.

_____

_____

_____

_____

_____

_____

_____

_____

_____

READING PART 2: *Underline the important information on the page, including the information in the box.*

Criminal Court Cases

A criminal case begins with the arrest of a person accused of committing a crime. The arrest is made by a law officer on the authority of a warrant, which is a written order or command issued by a court. However, if a police officer sees a crime being committed, he or she can arrest a person without a warrant. Usually there is a short examination of the evidence in a case before the real trial begins. The judge may then release the person charged, for lack of evidence, or may require the person to be held for investigation by a grand jury.

The grand jury (between 16 and 23 people) does not decide whether the person is guilty or innocent. It just decides whether there is enough evidence to indict the person. An indictment is a written statement charging the person with the crime. The accused person is then held in jail to wait for the trial or released on bail (payment of a large sum of money which will be lost if the person does not come to his trial at the correct time). The trial can result in a decision of mistrial if the jury can't decide on guilt or innocence (hung jury). The verdict of the jury can result in conviction (guilt) or acquittal (innocence). If the person is found guilty, the judge decides the sentence or penalty, which may be a fine, imprisonment, or both.

Degree of Proof Required

There is an important difference in the degree of proof required to win a civil lawsuit and the degree of proof required to win a criminal case. In order to convict a defendant of a criminal offense, the prosecutor must prove the facts "beyond a reasonable doubt." In other words, if the judge or jury is not overwhelmingly convinced of the defendant's guilt, the defendant must be acquitted. In a civil lawsuit, the plaintiff must prove his or her case "by preponderance of the evidence." This ordinarily means that the plaintiff's evidence simply must be more credible than the defendant's evidence. Thus the standard of proof is lower in civil cases and easier to achieve. This explains why a defendant may be acquitted of a crime (murder, assault, battery) and yet be liable to a plaintiff in a civil suit based on the same set of circumstances. In federal courts and in many state courts, the jury verdict must be unanimous. Some states, such as California, authorize a verdict in a civil action to be reached by vote of three-fourths of the jurors.

Appeals

After the entry of a judgment by the court, the party who feels dissatisfied by the outcome may file an appeal. Normally the loser appeals; sometimes the winner appeals (e.g., the plaintiff may allege that the damages awarded were inadequate under the evidence); occasionally both parties appeal.

In the cases you read about, the names of both parties are the title of the case. In criminal cases, the title may be The State v. Brown. If Brown sues Smith, the title will be Brown v. Smith. Brown is the plaintiff and Smith is the defendant. However, if Brown wins the case and Smith decides to appeal, the case will then have the title Smith v. Brown because Smith is now the plaintiff.

Reading Notes Part 2. Use the space below to take notes from the section of the text that is enclosed in a box. The information in your notes will be used to answer a question later.

_____

_____

_____

_____

_____

_____

_____

_____

_____

_____

Reading Summary Part 2:

Write a summary of the section in the box. Use your own words.

_____

_____

_____

_____

_____

_____

_____

_____

_____

_____

_____

2. Academic Vocabulary Building

Word Attack Skills. The more you know about word roots and endings (prefixes and suffixes), the easier it will be to read and learn new words.

More Noun suffixes.

Dr. Jones uses several nouns that have the ending **-ship**. This suffix signals that the word is a **noun** and the suffix can mean the state of something (how it is), the office, the profession, or the skill. Dr. Jones used these -ship words. What do these words mean?

citizenship

guardianship

dealership

Practice 2   -ship noun endings

→ **TASK**   Write new sentences by changing the **bolded** words into a noun with the suffix **-ship**.

Example:

I **own** that car.   The **ownership** papers are at home in my desk.

1. He is my business **partner**.

1. _____

2. I **relate** well to my parents.

2. _____

3. I think he is a good **friend**.

3. _____

4. Some local governments try to stop students from reading a book by **censoring** it.

4. _____

5. If you don't know academic language, it is **hard** to read textbooks.

5. _____

Other Prefixes, Suffixes, and Roots
used by Dr. Ida Jones:

Practice 3 Prefixes meaning negative, against, wrong, or opposite. Explain the meaning of the words below by using the prefix, root, and suffix to guess the meaning.

word	prefix, root, suffix	meaning?
dissatisfied	**dis** = not + **sat, satis** = enough	_____
misdemeanor	**mis** = wrong + **demeanor** = behavior	_____
mistrial	**mis** = wrong + **trial** = court procedure	_____
inadequate	**in**=not + **ad**=to + **equate**=make equal	_____
nonmonetary	**non**=not + **mone**=money + **ary**=relating to	_____
innocent	**in**=not + **noc, nox**=do harm	_____
controversy	**contro**=against + **vers**=to turn	_____

Words using other prefixes, suffixes and roots

unanimous	**uni**=one + **animus**=mind, soul	_____
credibility	**cred**=believe + **ibility**=able to	_____
juvenile	**juven**=young + **ile**=adjective ending	_____
convince	**con**=with + **vinc**=conquer	_____
certified	**cert**=understand clearly + **ify**=verb ending	_____
superior	**super, supra**=over, above	_____
supreme	**super, supra**=over, above	_____
alternative	**alter**=other + **ive**=noun ending	_____
testimony	**testare**=to witness + **mon**=advise, warn	_____
transcript	**trans**=across, over + **scrib, script**=write	_____

function	**funct**=perform + **tion**=noun ending	_____
confirm	**con**=with + **firm**=to make firm	_____
imprisonment	**im**=into + **prison**=jail + **ment**=noun ending	_____
nominate	**nomen**=to name + **ate**=cause something	_____
verdict	**ver**=true + **dic, dict**=say	_____
bankruptcy	**bank** + **rupt**=to break	_____
civil	**civ**=citizen +**il, ile**=capable of	_____
judgment	**ju, jud**=law, right + **ment**=noun ending	_____
jurisdiction	**jur**, **jus**=law, right + **dic, dict**=say	_____
justice	**jur, jus**=law, right + **ice**=noun ending	_____
litigation	**litig**=dispute + **ation**=noun form	_____
dysfunctional	**dys**=bad + **functional**=working	_____
circumstance	**circum**=around + **stance**=position	_____

Practice 4 Word Attack

➜ **TASK** Use your knowledge of roots, prefixes, and suffixes to understand and explain the following words. You can also look at lessons 1 and 2 to complete this exercise.

1. contradict   _____
2. civilian   _____
3. verify   _____
4. rejuvenate   _____
5. prejudice   _____
6. ruptured   _____
7. discredit   _____
8. misinform   _____
9. invincible   _____
10. misspell   _____

Latin Words and Phrases

Latin is the language that was used in ancient Rome. The language spread throughout Europe when the Roman Empire grew. Several modern languages evolved from Latin, including Spanish, Italian, and Portuguese. English has many technical, medical, legal, and academic words that are based on Latin or are Latin words and phrases. Latin used to be the language of scholarly learning. Many of the roots, prefixes, and suffixes we have studied are based on the Latin forms of the original words. In academic language, and especially in the language of the law, many Latin words and phrases are commonly used. Some of the words and phrases are used as abbreviations.

Latin Abbreviations and Phrases: Some Review, Some New

Latin Abbreviation	Latin Phrase	Meaning	Example
c.	circa	approximate date; we don't know the exact date	He died *c.* 1850.
cf	conferre	compare, bring together	Smith (1998) concluded that the idea is wrong (*cf* Jones 1996).
re	in re	about, concerning	He called *re* the meeting next week.
vs. or v.	versus	against	They studied the Brown *v.* Board of Education decision.
e.g.	exempli gratia	for example	People get the news in many ways (*e.g.* public radio).
i.e.	id est	that is	You should study academic vocabulary, *i.e.* the words used in textbooks.
n.b. or N.B.	nota bene	note, pay attention, 'note well'	*N.B.* The test is worth 50 points.
	[sic]	what came right before is a mistake that was made by the person who originally wrote the words.	They forgot to take there [*sic*] umbrellas.
R.I.P.	requiescat in pace	rest in peace - a phrase often said or written about someone who died	*R.I.P.* is sometimes written on a gravestone.
	ergo	therefore, hence	He committed a crime, *ergo* he must go to jail.

et al.	et alia	and the others, and the rest	Smith *et al.* wrote that book in 1980.
	ad hoc	temporary, for this time or for this purpose only	An *ad hoc* committee was formed to study the problem.
etc.	et cetera	and the rest	Don't forget to bring paper, pencil, ruler, *etc.*, to be ready for the class.
pro tem	pro tempore	for the time being, for now	He is president *pro tem* until the group elects a new leader.
ad lib	ad libitum	impromptu speech, speaking your own words if you forget what you are supposed to say in a speech or in a play	Some comedians *ad lib* when they see something funny in the audience.
	per se	because of its nature, in itself, intrinsically	It is not the money *per se* that keeps him working to help students.
	bona fide	genuine, sincere, real	It is a *bona fide* offer made by the company. You can get your money back if you are not satisfied.
	de facto	actual, in reality, real but not official	The barrio or ghetto is an example of *de facto* segregation.
	ex post facto	after the fact, done retroactively, later	The house was already built and the approval was gotten *ex post facto*.
	persona non grata	person who is not welcome, not acceptable	After he drank too much beer, he was *persona non grata* at the party.
	quid pro quo	an even or equal exchange	It was *quid pro quo*. I gave him the horse and he gave me the car.
	nolo contendere	no contest, guilt admitted	He pleaded *nolo contendere* to the speeding charge.
	in absentia	the person is absent	He could not attend the meeting so the award was given to him *in absentia*.

Practice 5 Latin Phrase Practice

→ **TASK** Explain the meaning of the **bolded** part of each sentence below.

1. The sign said, No Person Under 18 Are **[sic]** Allowed.

    _____

2. She was born **c.** 1902.

    _____

3. She speaks several languages, **e.g.** Hmong, Spanish, and French.

    _____

4. You should service your car this week, **i.e.**, change the oil, check the water, **etc.**

    _____

5. It wasn't just the food **per se**; she also went there for the music.

    _____

6. The book was written by Gonzalez **et al.** in 1958.

    _____

Word Forms Practice

Practice 6 Word Forms

→ **TASK** The following adjectives were used in Dr. Jones' lecture or reading. Work in small groups and use your knowledge or your dictionary to write the noun form of each word. Then use the adjective form OR the noun form in a short sentence.

adjective form	noun form	sentence
1. biased	_____	_____
		_____
2. hypothetical	_____	_____
		_____
3. unanimous	_____	_____
		_____

adjective form	noun form	sentence
4. guilty	_____	_____
		_____
5. innocent	_____	_____
		_____
6. negligent	_____	_____
		_____
7. suitable	_____	_____
		_____
8. complicated	_____	_____
		_____
9. controversial	_____	_____
		_____
10. appellate	_____	_____
		_____
11. just	_____	_____
		_____
12. liable	_____	_____
		_____
13. diverse	_____	_____
		_____
14. various	_____	_____
		_____
15. proven	_____	_____
		_____
16. alleged	_____	_____
		_____

Practice 7

➡ **TASK You Are the Lawyer!** Use the correct legal words from the list below to fill in the blanks. You can work in small groups, use your lecture notes, and use your reading notes.

1. trial	7. evidence	13. warrant	19. guilty
2. attorney	8. sentenced	14. bail	20. deposition
3. mistrial	9. witnesses	15. innocent	21. oath
4. indict	10. case	16. defendant	22. jurisdiction
5. sue	11. court	17. jury	23. fine
6. damages	12. plaintiff	18. civil	24. judge

Gus bought a used car from Sheila, but the car broke down after only one week. Gus decided to _____(A) Sheila for _____(B) . Gus called you because he needed a lawyer or an _____(C) to represent him in _____(D). First you had to decide which court had _____(E) over this case. This case is a _____(F) case because Gus, not the State, started the law suit. A _____(G) was issued for Sheila's arrest. The _____(H) looked at the _____(I) and decided that the _____(J) should go to the Grand Jury. The Grand Jury decided to _____(K) Sheila and she was arrested. However, she paid her _____(L) and was released until the time of the _____(M).

Prior to the trial, you contacted several _____(N) or people who knew Gus and knew about the car he bought from Sheila. Because some of those people could not come to Court during the trial, you interviewed them and videotaped their _____(O). During this interview, the witnesses had to speak under _____(P), which means they promised they were telling the truth.

When the trial started, Sheila was the _____(Q) and Gus was the _____(R). Twelve people were on the _____(S). Since you are the lawyer for Gus, you hope that the jury would decide that Sheila is _____(T). However, the jury might decide she is _____(U). Or, there might be a _____(V) if no decision can be reached by the jury. Fortunately, Sheila was found guilty of fraud and had to pay a _____(W) of $5,000. She was also _____(X) to six months in jail.

Practice 8   Trick Words   ✔✔✔

➜ **TASK** Trick Words are words or phrases that have a common meaning that you might know, but also have another meaning when used as academic vocabulary words. Use your dictionary to explain the following trick words as they were used in Lesson 3.

1. view _____

2. party _____

3. chief _____

4. degree _____

5. entitled _____

6. right _____

7. address _____

8. will _____

9. examination _____

10. file _____

11. relatively _____

12. simply _____

13. battery _____

14. case _____

15. damages _____

16. fine _____

17. just _____

18. sentence _____

Practice 9 Sentence Completion Practice

→ **TASK**   Work individually or in small groups to complete this exercise. These are sentences that Dr. Jones used in her lecture. Add the correct word endings in the blank space. Some blank spaces do not need anything added.   In order to do this exercise, you should be able to recognize what form of the word is being used in the sentence - noun, verb, adjective, or adverb.

1. Last year, the State_____ of California sue_____ or prosecute_____ the defend_____, the person who alleged_____ commit_____ the crime.

2. In a civil case_____, the injure_____ person control_____ the lawsuit_____.

3. On the certif_____ mail return receipt_____ card, you have to specif_____ who_____ is to receive_____ the summons.

4. One alternat_____ is to deliver_____ the summon_____ to the usual_____ place of residence to a person_____ of suitabl_____ age and discret_____.

5. If we assume_____ that the lawsuit_____ is going to be file_____ in Fresno, then that mean_____ that Gus would have to publish_____ notic_____ of it in the legal_____ newspaper in Fresno.

6. The Super_____ Court hear_____ civil_____ case_____ and felon_____ crimin_____ cases.

7. Specific_____ what we are go_____ to be look_____ at is how individual_____ get cases into court.

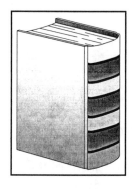

Part 3. Reading Skills and Strategies

In Lesson 2, you learned some reading strategies--things you can do to make reading easier and to be a better reader. We are going to practice these strategies again in a whole-class exercise on a passage about the Supreme Court that is on the next page (Practice 10).

Pre-reading

1. What is this about? (Look at the titles and subtitles). What do you know about the passage just from reading the subtitles? What do you already know about this topic? Thinking about what you know already will help you understand what you are reading. It is always easier to understand a topic if you know a little about it before you start reading.

2. What kinds of information will I see in this writing? As a group, make predictions about what kinds of information you will probably find in this passage. **Do not read anything except the subtitles before you make these predictions.**

3. Why am I reading this and what will I do with the information? If this is a college assignment, you will want to underline the important information and probably take notes. In this exercise you will be underlining the important information and you will decide sentence by sentence with the class what should be underlined.

During Reading

Each sentence should be read out loud one at a time by different students. Ask the following questions as you read:

1. How well did I understand this sentence? (Be honest!)
2. Are there any vocabulary words I am not sure of? If so, can I guess the meaning (see word attack skills, Lesson 1)?
3. Can I break this sentence into smaller parts or shorter sentences (see sentence complexity exercises in each lesson)?
4. Can I explain what this sentence means in my own words?
5. Should any of this be underlined because it is important information?
6. What is going to come next in the passage?

Post-reading

Close the book and as a whole class 'reconstruct' the passage on the board. Try to remember the subtitles and the important information in the passage. If you can't remember much, you did not really understand the passage and your self-monitoring was not working.

Practice 10 Pre-reading, During-reading, and Post-reading Practice

The Supreme Court

Appellate Function

The chief function of the Supreme Court is its appellate function. Most of the cases it reviews come from the courts of appeals, although a few come from other federal courts and even from the highest state courts. Even though the highest appellate courts of the states are not part of the federal court system *per se*, they may have their decisions appealed to the Supreme Court when the issue in the case involves a federal question.

Discretion on Choice of Cases

A litigant (litigants are the parties in dispute) is not entitled as a matter of right to be heard in the United States Supreme Court. This is true even if a case involves a federal question. The Supreme Court has discretion to choose only the cases it deems most important to hear.

The Justices

The judges or members of the Supreme Court are called "justices." The Constitution is silent about the size of the Supreme Court, and the number of justices has varied between six and ten. It is now, and for many years has been, nine. There is no constitutional requirement that a person be a judge, or even a lawyer, to be appointed to the Supreme Court. One of the justices is elected Chief Justice and the rest are Associate Justices.

Justices are nominated by the President but must be confirmed by the Senate before they are appointed for life terms. Because the appointment is for life, the decision of whom to appoint is very important and the Senate often rejects the person nominated by the President. Of course, most people nominated by a president will be people who agree with his political views.

4. Sentence Complexity

Long sentences are often made up of smaller sentences hooked together with connectors. The words and phrases we are calling connectors are listed in your dictionary for each lesson. The connectors are very important for understanding the meaning of what you are reading. In this lesson we will practice with some of the connectors.

Practice 11   Connectors

➜ **TASK** Use your dictionary from lessons 1, 2, and this lesson to see what these connectors mean and how they are used. Then put the two short sentences together with the connector provided.   Example:

rather than   Gus bought a used car. Gus did not buy a new car.
                          <u>Gus bought a used car rather than a new car.</u>

1. **in order to**   Gus wants to sue Sheila. But first he has to get a lawyer.

_____

2. **otherwise**   In small claims court Gus does not need a lawyer. In any other court he does.

_____

3. **even though**   The car broke down. Sheila had said it was in good condition.

_____

4. **however**   In a civil case you need a lawyer. In small claims court you don't.

_____

5. **not only ... but ... also** The transmission broke. The motor burned up.

_____

6. **in contrast to**   Civil cases are controlled by the injured party. Criminal cases are controlled by the State.

_____

7. **whether or not**   You can get divorced if your spouse is present. You can get divorced if your spouse is missing.

_____

8. **in fact**   Dr. Jones had to pass the bar exam to practice law. She passed the bar in three states.

_____

9. **either...or**   Gus can sue Sheila in small claims court. Gus can sue Sheila in a civil court.

_____

5. Academic Culture

Law School

A person who is qualified to practice law is called a lawyer or attorney. In England, they are also called barristers or solicitors. In the U.S., a student must first graduate from college with a bachelor's degree before entering law school. Law school takes a minimum of three years of study to complete. Law schools are often part of a university, but they may also be separate public or private schools. Dr. Jones has a law degree (Juris Doctorate, J.D.) from New York University.

Graduating from a law school is the first step to being able to practice law. After graduation, a student must also pass the bar exam for any state in which she wishes to practice. Each state has different laws and a different bar exam. The bar exams are very difficult and many people have to take them more than once. Some people never pass. Dr. Jones has passed the bar exam in New York, Nebraska, and California.

Academic Legal Issues: Patents, Copyright, and Plagiarism

When someone invents a new procedure or machine, he or she can **patent** it. Patenting something means that the owner or inventor has legally registered the idea or invention with the government and he or she now has legal control over how the idea or invention is used, produced, and sold.   The person who holds the patent makes money when the item he patented is produced and sold. Many times when a successful new idea or invention is made, a lot of lawyers are involved in determining who should have the patent. Sometimes these legal fights can take years to resolve. Some lawyers specialize in patent law.

For writing and music, a **copyright** is the legal equivalent to a **patent**. When you see the symbol © , this means that the written material or music is protected under the copyright laws. Only the person who created the original writing or music has a right to make money from the sale of the writing or music. If anybody uses the words or music without permission of the author or composer, there can be legal problems.

If you want to use the words of another person, you need to use "quotation marks" to show which words belong to another person, and tell the reader the page number, the name of the book, and the author who wrote these words. If you use another person's ideas, you must also tell where the ideas originally came from.

One of the reasons that you need to learn to take notes from your reading and to write information in your own words is because using someone else's words is illegal. It is like stealing because the words are copyrighted. All colleges and universities have rules against **plagiarism** or copying someone else's words verbatim (word for word). If you copy words from a book and claim that the words are your own writing, you can receive a grade of F in a class and you can even be expelled from school. **Plagiarism** is a very serious academic problem! In Lesson 1, you also read about the problem of plagiarism (see p. 34).

ALADIN Dictionary Lesson 3

Table of Contents

1. Thinking   Page 155

2. Person Characteristics   Page 156

3. Importance   Page 158

4. Information   Page 159

5. Research, Academic   Page 161

6. Cause-effect, Change   Page 162

7. Hedge, Qualify   Page 165

8. History, Government, Society   Page 166

9. Time   Page 171

10. Connectors and Comparisons   Page 172

11. Evaluation and Description   Page 173

Alphabetical list of Words/Phrases and Page Numbers in Lesson 3 Dictionary

Word/Phrase	Page
abbreviated	173
accuse	155
achieve	162
acquittal	162
	166
address ✔	159
administration	166
alimony	166
allege	155
	165
alternative ✂	159
anticipate	155
	171
appeal	162
appellate	166
assault	166
at times	171
attach ✔	162
attorney	166
authority	166
bail	166
bailiff	166
bankruptcy ✂	166
basic	159
battery ✔	167
biased	155
breach	162
case ✔	167
category	160
certificate ✂	158
charge ✔	167
chief ✔	158
child support	167
circumstance ✂	162
civil ✂	167
civil procedure ✂	167
collide	162
complaint ✔	167
complicated	160
concise	160
confirm ✂	162
	167
constable	156
constitute ✔	160
Constitution	167
contract	167
controversy ✂	155
	160
	162
conviction ✂	162
	167
convince ✂	155
	156
counsel	167
credibility ✂	156
criminal	156
damages ✔	168

Word/Phrase	Page
declaration	168
deem	173
defendant	156
	168
degree ✔	158
deposition	160
	168
discretion ✔	157
	168
dispute	160
	162
dissatisfied ✂	157
dissolution	162
distinction	161
diversity	173
doubt	155
due process ✂	168
encourage ✂	163
entitled ✔	158
equity	173
establish	163
evaluate	173
even though	172
evidence	160
	161
	168
examination ✔	161
fault	163
federal	168
felony	168
file ✔	163
fine ✔	168
for life	172
fraud	160
	163
fresh ✔	173
function ✂	161
grand ✔	158
guilty	157
gullible	157
have it delivered	163
hear ✔	169
however	172
hypothetical	155
implied	165
imprisonment ✂	163
	169
in order to	172
in the case of	165
in essence	165
inadequate ✂	173
indict	169
indictment	163
initially ✔	172
initiate	163
injunction	163
innocent ✂	157
interstate ✂	169
issue	160
judgment ✂	163
	169
jurisdiction ✂	169
juror	169

Word/Phrase	Page
justice ✂	169
juvenile ✂	157
lack	158
lawsuit	169
liable	169
lien ✔	163
limited	165
litigation ✂	169
misdemeanor ✂	169
mistrial ✂	170
municipal	170
negligent	157
nominate ✂	164
	170
nonmonetary ✂	174
oath	155
obviously	156
occasionally	172
offense ✔	170
opposing	172
order ✔	170
ordinarily ✔	165
	172
otherwise	172
outcome ✂	164
overwhelmingly	159
party ✔	157
per se	165
	173
petition ✔	170
plaintiff	170
plea bargain ✔	164
preponderance	159
preserve	164
prior	172
probate	170
procedure	161
	164
process server	157
proof	160
	170
proposed ✔	156
prosecute	170
prosecutor	170
rather than	173
real property ✔	170
reasonable	159
receipt	160
reject ✂	164
relatively ✔	165
relief ✔	164
remark ✔	160
remedy	164
request	164
resolve	164
right ✔	159
root ✔	161
sentence ✔	171
shady ✔	157
sheriff	157
simply ✔	164

Word/Phrase	Page
solution	164
specifically	165
spouse	157
standard	158
statute	171
sufficient	174
suitable	158
summons	171
superior ✂	159
supreme ✂	159
synonymous	173
take possession of	164
testimony ✂	161
	171
theoretically	165
transcript ✂	161
tribunal	171
try ✔	171
ultimately	172
unanimous ✂	156
	159
under oath	165
usually	172
various	174
variously	165
verdict ✂	164
	171
victim	158
view ✔	156
violation	171
warrant	171
warranty	161
will ✔	161

1. Thinking

Noun	Verb	Adjective	Adverb	Definition	Example
accusation accuser	**accuse**	accused accusatory	accusingly	v. blame, charge, tell someone they did something bad	A criminal case begins with the arrest of a person **accused** of committing a crime.
allegation	**allege**	alleged	allegedly	v. claim something is true; claim somebody is guilty	The plaintiff may **allege** that the damages awarded were inadequate.
anticipation	**anticipate**	anticipatory		v. think about something that will happen in the future, look forward to	The teaching experience is not one I initially **anticipated**.
bias	bias	**biased**		adj. not a neutral opinion - either for something or against something, not fair	There was a fear that state courts might be **biased** toward residents of their own state.
controversy ✂		controversial	controversial-ly	n. disagreement about something; when people do not agree	Cases are heard in Small Claims Court as long as the amount of the **controversy** is $5,000 or less.
	convince ✂	convincing	convincingly	v. make somebody believe something or get him to do something by talking to him and persuading him	The lawyer must **convince** the jury that her client is innocent.
doubt	doubt	doubtful	doubtfully	n. not sure something is true, don't believe it is true	The prosecutor must prove the facts beyond reasonable **doubt**.
hypothesis	hypothesize	**hypotheti-cal**	hypothetically	adj. theoretical, imaginary, unproven	The court ordinarily will not answer **hypothetical** questions.
oath				n. words you say when you promise or swear that something is true	Witnesses must take an **oath** stating that what they say is true.

Noun	Verb	Adjective	Adverb	Definition	Example
obviousness	obviate	obvious	**obviously**	adv. can be easily seen or understood, clear to everyone	Gus does not want to make the payments, **obviously** because the car was bad before he bought it.
proposal proposition	propose	**proposed** ✔		adj. suggested, intended, planned, not yet made or done	The court will not advise what a person's rights would be under a **proposed** contract.
unanimity		**unanimous** ✂	unanimously	adj. everyone agrees, total agreement	In federal courts the jury verdict must be **unanimous**.
view ✔	view			n. opinion, attitude, belief	Of course most people nominated by a president will be people who agree with his political **views**.

2. Person Characteristics

Noun	Verb	Adjective	Adverb	Definition	Example
	convince ✂	convincing	convincingly	v. make somebody believe something or get him to do something by talking to him and persuading him	The jury must be overwhelmingly **convinced** of the defendant's guilt.
constable constabulary				n. another name for a police officer	He can give her notice of the suit by having a **constable** deliver a summons.
credibility ✂		credible	credibly	n. person who has credibility can be believed, seems honest	The judge and jury can see the witness and evaluate the person's **credibility**.
criminal crime criminology criminologist		**criminal**	criminally	adj. broke the law, committed a crime	In a **criminal** case, the victim does not control the case.
defendant defense defender	defend	defensive	defensively	n. person who is charged or accused of the crime, the person who must defend himself	A summons is delivered to the **defendant**.

Noun	Verb	Adjective	Adverb	Definition	Example
discretion		discretionary		n. correct, careful thinking or decision-making	The summons must be delivered to someone of suitable age and **discretion**.
dissatisfac-tion		**dissatisfied** ✂ dissatisfac-tory	dissatisfac-torily	adj. not happy, does not have what he wants, does not have enough	The party who feels **dissatisfied** by the outcome may file an appeal.
guilt		**guilty**	guiltily	adj. did something wrong, not innocent	The grand jury does not decide whether a person is **guilty** or innocent.
gullibility		**gullible**	gullibly	adj. a person who will believe anything, even stupid things	**Gullible** Gus bought a car from Shady Sheila.
innocence		**innocent** ✂	innocently	adj. did not do anything wrong, not guilty	The grand jury does not decide whether a person is guilty or **innocent**.
juvenile		**juvenile** ✂		adj. young person, not an adult yet	**Juvenile** court cases also go to the Superior Court.
negligence	neglect	**negligent**	negligently	adj. not responsible, not careful, causing problems	The defendant drove his automobile in a **negligent** manner.
party ✔				n. person involved in a lawsuit, participant in lawsuit	The function of a court is to decide controversies between **parties** in a lawsuit.
process server				n. person who delivers court summons	You can have the sheriff or a **process server** or someone like that actually deliver the summons.
		shady ✔		adj. not completely honest, of bad character	Gullible Gus bought a car from **Shady** Sheila.
sheriff				n. police officer in a rural or county area, not in a city	A **sheriff** or process server or someone like that actually delivers the summons.
spouse		spousal		n. person you are married to, husband or wife	Sometimes one **spouse** is totally absent and there is no way to locate him or her.

Noun	Verb	Adjective	Adverb	Definition	Example
standard standardi-zation	standardize	standard standardized		n. the normal amount, the necessary amount, the amount you compare everything else to	The **standard** of proof is lower in civil cases and is easier to achieve.
suitability		**suitable**	suitably	adj. right, correct, appropriate	The summons must be delivered to someone of **suitable** age and discretion.
victim victimization	victimize	victimized		n. the person who was hurt or robbed in a crime	You still have a **victim** in a criminal case, but the **victim** does not control the case, the state does.

3. Importance

Noun	Verb	Adjective	Adverb	Definition	Example
certificate ✂ certification	certify	**certified** ✂ certifiable certificated	certifiably	n. short paper or document that shows something is true adj. shown to be true, correct, valid	You get a little green **certificate** back when you send something by **certified** mail.
chief		**chief** ✔	chiefly	adj. most important	The **chief** function of the Supreme Court is its appellate function.
degree ✔				n. amount, how much, extent	There is an important difference in the **degree** of proof required to win a civil lawsuit.
entitlement	entitle	**entitled** ✔		adj. have the right to do something	A litigant is not **entitled** as a matter of right to be heard in the Supreme Court.
		grand ✔		adj. great, important	The **grand** jury does not decide whether a person is guilty or innocent.
lack	lack	lacking		n. not enough, deficient	The judge may release the person for **lack** of evidence.

Noun	Verb	Adjective	Adverb	Definition	Example
	overwhelm	overwhelming	**overwhel-mingly**	adv. a lot extra, more than minimum, a huge amount	The jury must be **overwhelmingly** convinced of the defendant's guilt.
preponder-ance		preponderant		n. most, more than half, more than enough	In a civil lawsuit the plaintiff must prove his case by a **preponderance** of the evidence.
reason	reason	**reasonable**	reasonably	adj. logical, correct amount, appropriate amount	The prosecutor must prove the facts beyond a **reasonable** doubt.
right ✔				n. the power to do something, the privilege to do something	A litigant is not entitled as a matter of **right** to be heard in the Supreme Court.
superiority		**superior** ✂		adj. better, higher	The next level of the California system is the **Superior** Court system.
supremacy		**supreme** ✂	supremely	adj. highest or greatest	The highest court in the federal court system is of course the **Supreme** Court.
unanimity		**unanimous** ✂	unanimously	adj. everyone agrees; total agreement	In federal courts the jury verdict must be **unanimous**.

4. Information

Noun	Verb	Adjective	Adverb	Definition	Example
address	**address** ✔			v. talk to a group	The judge may tell an attorney to **address** his remarks to the court.
alternative ✂	alternate	alternative	alternatively alternately	n. other way of doing something, another choice	One **alternative** is to deliver her certified mail to the usual place of residence.
basis	base	**basic**	basically	adj. simplest form, fundamental, elementary	There are two **basic** court systems, federal and state.

Noun	Verb	Adjective	Adverb	Definition	Example
category	categorize	categorical	categorically	n. a particular kind or class of something	There is a special **category** of federal cases that deal with state citizenship.
complication	complicate	**complicated**		adj. complex, not simple, not easy to understand	The court has to have jurisdiction over the subject matter and that is a more **complicated** issue.
		concise	concisely	adj. short, clear, just the necessary amount of information, not extra information	The complaint must be in ordinary and **concise** language.
constitution	**constitute** ✔	constitutional	constitution-ally	v. made of, combining to make something	The complaint must contain a statement of the facts **constituting** the cause of action.
controversy ✀		controversial	controver-sially	n. disagreement about something	The main function of a court is to decide **controversies** between parties in a lawsuit.
deposition	depose			n. testimony; speak about something, promising to tell the truth	A **deposition** is a statement under oath made at a hearing.
dispute	dispute	disputed disputing		n. disagreement, argument	The court's main function is to resolve **disputes**.
evidence		evident	evidently	n. information that shows something is true, supports the idea	The plaintiff must prove his or her case by preponderance of **evidence**.
fraud fraudulence	defraud	fraudulent	fraudulently	n. get something dishonestly, by lying	He is suing her for **fraud** because he is arguing that she lied about this whole situation.
issue				n. problem, controversy	Other kinds of federal cases involve Civil Rights **issues**.
proof	prove	proven		n. information or evidence to show something is true	Certified mail provides **proof** that the notice has been received.
receipt receiver reception	receive	receivable reception		n. paper or document showing you got something	With certified mail you get a return **receipt** of a little green card.
remark ✔	remark			n. something you say, comment on, talk	The judge may tell an attorney to address his **remarks** to the court.

Noun	Verb	Adjective	Adverb	Definition	Example
root ✔		root		n. origin, where something came from	Litigation comes to us from a Latin **root** meaning dispute.
testimony ✂	testify	testimonial		n. speak about something in court	The lawyers on each side discover what the **testimony** will be.
transcript ✂ transcription	transcribe	transcribed		n. a written copy of what someone said	A court reporter prepares a written **transcript** of the questions and answers.
warranty				n. guarantee, promise that something is good or working well	An implied breach of **warranty** says that she promised that the car would at least run.
will ✔	will			n. a legal paper or document that says what should happen to your money and property after you die	Probate cases relate to transfer of property under a **will**.

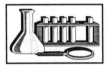

5. Research, Academic

Noun	Verb	Adjective	Adverb	Definition	Example
distinction	distinguish [between]	distinct distinctive	distinctly	n. the difference between two things	I gave you the **distinction** between a civil case and a criminal case.
evidence		evident	evidently	n. information that shows something is true, supports the idea	Usually there is a short examination of the **evidence** before the trial.
examination ✔	examine			n. inspection, looking closely at something	Usually there is a short **examination** of the evidence before the trial.
function ✂	function	functional	functionally	n. purpose of the activity, duty, or work	The chief **function** of the Supreme Court is its appellate function.
procedure	proceed	procedural	procedurally	n. way of doing something, what happens next	**Procedures** prior to trial may include depositions.

6. Cause-Effect, Change

Noun	Verb	Adjective	Adverb	Definition	Example
achievement achiever	**achieve**			v. get something, reach a goal	The standard of proof is lower in civil cases and easier to **achieve**.
acquittal	acquit	acquitted		n. the court decides that the defendant is not guilty, is innocent of charges	The verdict can result in conviction (guilt) or **acquittal** (innocence).
appeal	appeal	appellate		n. requesting or asking the court to consider the case and decision again	The party who feels dissatisfied by the outcome may file an **appeal**.
	attach ✔			v. legally take something to settle a debt	The attorney may try to **attach** her car dealership.
breach	breach	breached		n. violation of promise or contract, did not do what he agreed to do or promised to do	There has been a **breach** of contract and maybe fraud.
circumstance ✂		circumstantial		n. person's position, what's happening around a person	A plaintiff may be liable in a civil suit based on the same set of **circumstances**.
collision	**collide**			v. crash, bump into	The defendant's automobile **collided** with the plaintiff's.
confirmation	**confirm** ✂	confirmed confirmatory		v. approve officially	Justices are nominated by the President but **confirmed** by the Senate.
controversy ✂		controversial	controver-sially	n. disagreement, dispute	The main function of the court is to decide **controversies** between parties in a lawsuit.
conviction ✂ convict	convict	convicted		n. court says a person is guilty	The verdict can result in **conviction** (guilt) or acquittal (innocence).
dispute	dispute	disputed disputing		n. disagreement, argument	Litigation comes to us from the Latin root meaning **dispute**.
dissolution	dissolve	dissolved		n. the end, breaking apart	In a case of **dissolution** action, someone is filing for divorce.

Noun	Verb	Adjective	Adverb	Definition	Example
encourage-ment	**encourage** ✄	encouraging	encour-agingly	v. give support, give courage to do something, praise	Many courts have **encouraged** the use of videotape depositions.
establishment	**establish**	established		v. make something new, create, form	Usually, however, court means a tribunal **established** by the state.
fault	fault	faulty	faultily	n. the one to blame, the one who did something wrong	If you are in a car accident and you are not at **fault**, you might sue the person who hit you.
	file ✔			v. to bring a lawsuit before a court	In a dissolution action, someone is **filing** for divorce.
fraud fraudulence	defraud	fraudulent	fraudulently	n. lie to and cheat someone, trick someone, take money	There has been a breach of contract and maybe **fraud.**
	have it delivered			v. cause it to happen, get somebody to do it for you	You can give notice of the suit by **having the summons delivered**.
imprisonment ✄	imprison	imprisoned		n. being put into prison	The judge decides the sentence or penalty, which may be a fine or **imprisonment**, or both.
indictment	indict	indicted		n. formal statement that a person is charged with a crime	An **indictment** is a written statement charging the person with the crime.
initiative initiation	**initiate** ✔	initial	initially	v. begin, start	The party who **initiates** the civil suit is called the plaintiff.
injunction	enjoin			n. a court order that says you must do something or stop doing something	You can sue in Superior Court to get an **injunction** so that the neighbor has to stop the dog from barking.
judgment	judge	judged judgmental	judgmen-tally	n. decision about something, decision about whether it is good or bad, right or wrong	The court's decision is called a **judgment**.
lien ✔				n. a legal claim to someone's property	To attach her dealership means to put a **lien** on it.

Noun	Verb	Adjective	Adverb	Definition	Example
nomination nominee	**nominate** ✂			v. suggested person, proposed person, named person	Justices are **nominated** by the President.
outcome ✂				n. result, how something happens in the end	The party who feels dissatisfied by the **outcome** may file an appeal.
plea bargain ✔				n. an agreement that if a person pleads guilty, then he will get a lighter sentence	It is the prosecutor or the state who decides if someone is going to get a **plea bargain**.
preservation	**preserve**	preserved		v. save something so that it is never lost or destroyed	One purpose of a deposition is to **preserve** the testimony.
procedure	proceed	procedural	procedural-ly	n. way of doing something; how it is done	In order to get a case into a court, you have to follow a certain **procedure**.
rejection	**reject** ✂	rejected		v. say no, get rid of something	The Senate often **rejects** the person nominated by the President.
relief ✔	relieve	relieved		n. award of money to the innocent person or giving of punishment to the guilty person	The complaint includes a demand of the **relief** which the plaintiff claims.
remedy	remedy	remedial		n. solution or answer to a problem	Equity involves suing for some **remedy** other than for money.
request requisition	**request**	requested		v. ask for	The plaintiff would then **request** damages.
resolution	**resolve**	resolute resolved	resolutely	v. solve, find an agreement, get people to agree	The court's main function is to **resolve** disputes.
solution	solve	solvable		n. the answer to a problem	If someone has disappeared, the law has a **solution** for that.
	take possession of			v. take something legally	The sheriff might **take possession of** those cars that she owns.
verdict ✂				n. decision of the jury	The **verdict** can result in conviction (guilt) or acquittal (innocence).

7. Hedge, Qualify

Hedge Word or Phrase	Explanation	Example
allege	say something is true, but with no proof; assert	The plaintiff may **allege** that the damages awarded were inadequate.
implied	not stated directly; implicit, not explicit	Gus filed suit for an **implied** breach of warranty; he thought there was a promise the car would at least work.
in essence	essentially, really, actually, for the most part	To attach her dealership means, **in essence**, placing a lien on the dealership so she can't sell it.
in the case of	when this particular thing happens	**In the case of** a dissolution action, sometimes one spouse is totally absent.
limited	not complete, not total	Some courts have **limited** jurisdiction.
ordinarily	usually, most of the time	This **ordinarily** means that the plaintiff's evidence simply must be more credible.
per se	by itself, as such, intrinsically	Even though the highest state appellate courts are not part of the federal court system **per se**, they may have their decisions appealed to the Supreme Court.
relatively ✔	compared to other things, relative to other things	A summons is a **relatively** small piece of paper.
simply ✔	only this, nothing more	This ordinarily means that the plaintiff's evidence **simply** must be more credible.
specifically	exactly the part we are looking at	**Specifically** what we are looking at today is how individuals get cases into court.
theoretically	could happen, might happen, in theory	Publication in the legal newspaper means that **theoretically** the spouse can see it.
under oath	swear in court with your hand on a Bible that you will tell the whole truth and nothing but the truth, so help you God	A deposition is a statement **under oath**.
variously	called by several different names	The plaintiff files with the court what is **variously** called a complaint, petition, or declaration.

8. History, Government, Society

Noun	Verb	Adjective	Adverb	Definition	Example
acquittal	acquit	acquitted		n. verdict or decision of not guilty	The verdict can result in conviction (guilt) or **acquittal** (innocence).
administra-tion administrator	administer	administrative	administratively	n. management, control over	A court is established for the **administration** of justice.
alimony				n. money paid every month by one spouse to another after divorce	The court can't order **alimony** or child support without jurisdiction over the person.
appeal	appeal	**appellate**		adj. the adjective of appeal, ask for some thing to be reconsidered	The chief function of the Supreme court is its **appellate** function.
assault	assault	assaulted		n. a violent attack, or a threat to hurt someone	The defendant may be acquitted of a crime such as murder, **assault**, or battery.
attorney				n. lawyer; a person who represents you in legal matters, also attorney-at-law	The judge tells an **attorney** to address his or her remarks to the court.
authority	authorize	authoritative	authoritatively	n. legal control, the person or office in charge of something	The arrest is made by a law officer on the **authority** of a warrant.
bail	bail out			n. money you pay to stay out of jail while you wait for your trial	The accused person is held in jail to wait for the trial or released on **bail**.
bailiff				n. officer who makes sure people behave correctly in court	A **bailiff** keeps order in the court.
bankruptcy ✂	bankrupt declare bankruptcy	bankrupt		n. legally saying you have no money to pay debts	**Bankruptcy** cases involve federal laws.

Noun	Verb	Adjective	Adverb	Definition	Example
battery ✔	batter	battered		n. the act of hurting, battering, beating someone	The defendant may be acquitted of a crime such as murder, assault, or **battery**.
case ✔				n. lawsuit	Most of the **cases** come from the courts of appeals.
charge	**charge** ✔	charged		v. saying what the person did wrong or did illegally	An indictment is a written statement **charging** the person with the crime.
child support				n. money paid each month by a parent after a divorce to take care of the children	The court can't order alimony or **child support** without jurisdiction over the person.
civil procedure civil case ✄				n. not a criminal case; relating to the rights of citizens under civil laws	In a **civil procedure**, the injured person controls the lawsuit.
civilian civilization	civilize	**civil** ✄		adj. about private citizens, not military, not religious	**Civil** rights laws are federal laws.
complaint ✔				n. the information about the case that starts the lawsuit	The plaintiff initiates a lawsuit by filing a **complaint**.
confirmation	**confirm**	confirmed confirmatory		v. agree with the decision	Justices are nominated by the President but **confirmed** by the Senate.
Constitution		Constitutional		n. the document that states the basic laws of the US government	The U.S. **Constitution** says if you want to sue somebody you have to give them notice.
contract contractor	contract with	contractual	contractually	n. written agreement between two parties	The court will not advise a person about his rights in a proposed **contract**.
conviction convict	convict	convicted		n. verdict or decision of guilty	The verdict can result in **conviction** (guilt) or acquittal (innocence).
counsel				n. another name for lawyer, attorney	The judge says not to address comments to the opposing **counsel**.

Noun	Verb	Adjective	Adverb	Definition	Example
damages ✔				n. the penalty of money that the guilty person pays to the victim or injured person	The plaintiff would then request **damages** in a certain amount, such as $100,000.
declaration	declare			n. the information about the case that starts the lawsuit	The plaintiff initiates a lawsuit by filing a **declaration**.
defendant defender defense	defend	defensive	defensively	n. person accused of the crime in a court case, must defend himself	The summons has to be delivered to the **defendant**.
deposition	depose			n. information a person gives before a trial begins; the person swears it is the truth	A **deposition** is a statement under oath made at a hearing.
discretion		discretionary		n. power to choose, the right to choose	The Supreme Court has **discretion** to choose only the cases it deems important to hear.
due process				n. under the 14th Amendment of the Constitution, a person has the right to due process or correct and fair treatment under the law	If you are arguing that **due process** has been violated, then that is a federal issue.
evidence		evident	evidently	n. information and things collected that show that the defendant is either guilty or innocent	Usually there is a short examination of the **evidence** in a case before the real trial begins.
federation		**federal**		adj. a union of states under a central government	We are going to talk about the State court system and the **Federal** court system.
felony felon		felonious		n. a serious crime; worse than a misdemeanor	The Superior Court hears **felony** criminal cases which are the more serious criminal cases.
fine ✔	fine			n. money paid as punishment for being guilty	The sentence may be a **fine**, imprisonment, or both.

Noun	Verb	Adjective	Adverb	Definition	Example
hearing	hear ✔			v. the process of a case being in court; the judge and jury listens to or hears the case	We are looking at how individuals get cases into court and **heard** by a judge.
		interstate ✄		adj. between states, from state to state	We do a lot of business **interstate** and we travel **interstate** a lot.
imprison-ment ✄	imprison	imprisoned		n. being put in prison	The sentence may be a fine, **imprisonment**, or both.
indictment	indict	indicted		v. bring a person to trial, formally charge the person with a crime	The grand jury decides whether there is enough evidence to **indict** the person.
judgment ✄	judge adjudicate	judicial judicious judgmental	judicially judiciously judgmentally	n. a decision in court	The court's decision is called a **judgment**.
jurisdiction ✄		jurisdictional		n. the authority or power to interpret the law, area of legal power	We have to determine first what court has **jurisdiction** over the lawsuit.
juror jury				n. a person on the jury	California authorizes a verdict in a civil action to be reached by vote of three-fourths of the **jurors**.
justice ✄		just ✔	justly	n. correct, fair treatment under the law	A court is established for the administration of **justice**.
lawsuit				n. a case in court	In a civil procedure, the injured person controls the **lawsuit**.
liability		liable		adj. responsible for the problem	The defendant may be **liable** to a plaintiff in a civil suit.
litigation ✄ litigant	litigate	litigious	litigiously	n. lawsuit	A court decides controversies between parties in a lawsuit (the **litigation**).
misdemean-or ✄				n. a less serious crime; not a felony (serious crime)	In a **misdemeanor** case the maximum time in jail is one year.

169

Noun	Verb	Adjective	Adverb	Definition	Example
mistrial ✂				n. the trial ended in no decision or verdict; the jury can't agree	The trial can result in a decision of **mistrial** if the jury can't decide on guilt or innocence.
municipality		**municipal**	municipally	adj. relating to the city or local government, not state or federal	**Municipal** Courts are what most cities have.
nomination nominee	**nominate** ✂			v. suggest a person for a job, position, or office	Justices are **nominated** by the President.
offense ✔	offend	offensive	offensively	n. the crime, what the person did wrong	In order to convict a person of a criminal **offense**, the prosecutor must prove the facts.
order ✔	order	orderly		n. correct or proper behavior	A bailiff keeps **order** in the court.
petition ✔	petition			n. the information about the case that starts the lawsuit	The plaintiff initiates a lawsuit by filing a **petition**.
plaintiff				n. the person who files the civil suit against another person	The **plaintiff** filed a suit against the defendant.
probate				n. the process of showing that a person's will is legal and valid	**Probate** cases relate to a transfer of property under a will.
proof	prove	proven		n. evidence, information to show something is true	There is an important difference in the degree of **proof** required to win a civil lawsuit.
prosecutor prosecution	prosecute	prosecuted		n. lawyer who works for the state and tries to prove that the defendant is guilty of the crime	In order to convict a person of a criminal offense, the **prosecutor** must prove the facts.
prosecutor prosecution	**prosecute**	prosecuted		v. sue in a court, begin and continue a lawsuit	The State of California sues or **prosecutes** the defendant.
real property ✔				n. buildings and/or land, real estate	She has some cars on the lot but she doesn't actually own the **real property**.

Noun	Verb	Adjective	Adverb	Definition	Example
sentence ✔	sentence			n. decision of what punishment the guilty person should get	The judge decides the **sentence** or penalty.
statute		statutory		n. written law	There is a federal **statute** that says a civil rights violation is a federal case.
summons	summon			n. an order to come to and appear in court on a certain day	Now a **summons** is just a piece of paper that says you have been sued.
testimony ✂	testify	testimonial		n. information a person gives during a court case; the person swears it is true	The lawyers on each side discover what the **testimony** will be.
trial	try ✔			v. having a trial; have a case decided in court	First the officers were **tried** under federal law.
tribunal				n. a court of justice	A court is a **tribunal** established by the State.
verdict ✂				n. decision of the jury	The **verdict** of the jury can result in conviction or acquittal.
violation	violate	violated		n. breaking of a law or rule	**Violations** of civil rights laws are federal issues.
warrant				n. official paper issued by a court that says a person should be arrested	The arrest is made by a law officer on the authority of a **warrant**.

9. Time

Noun or Expression	Verb	Adjective	Adverb	Definition	Example
anticipation	**anticipate**	anticipatory		v. think about something that will happen in the future	The teaching experience is not one I initially **anticipated**.
at times				sometimes	**At times**, the word court is synonymous with judge.

Noun or Expression	Verb	Adjective	Adverb	Definition	Example
for life				all your life; as long as you live	Supreme Court justices are appointed **for life**.
initial	initiate	initial	**initially** ✔	adv. in the beginning, at first	The teaching experience is not one I **initially** anticipated.
		ordinary	**ordinarily** ✔	adv. most of the time, usually	**Ordinarily** the court will not answer hypothetical questions.
occasion		occasional	**occasionally** on occasion	adv. sometimes, not too often	**Occasionally** both parties appeal a decision.
priority	prioritize	**prior**		adj. earlier, what came before	Several procedures occur **prior** to trial.
		ultimate	**ultimately**	adv. finally, in the end	**Ultimately** it is the prosecutor or the state who decides whether to go to trial.
		usual	**usually**	adv. most of the time, often	**Usually** the word court means a tribunal established by the state.

10. Connectors and Comparisons

Connector	Meaning	Example
even though	although	**Even though** the highest state appellate courts are not part of the federal court system per se, they may have their decisions appealed to the Supreme Court.
however	but	Usually, **however**, court means a tribunal established by the state.
in order to	to get A (conviction), you must do B first (prove the facts)	**In order to** convict a defendant, the prosecutor must prove the facts.
opposing	the lawyer on the other side of the case, the opposition	An attorney should address her remarks to the court, not to the **opposing** counsel.
otherwise	if not, or else, on the other hand	He could go to Small Claims Court. **Otherwise**, he could hire a lawyer and go to the Civil Municipal Court.

Connector	Meaning	Example
per se	not exactly; not really	Even though the highest state appellate courts are not part of the federal court system **per se**, they may have their decisions appealed to the Supreme Court.
rather than	instead of, in place of	Today I am going to focus on civil cases **rather than** criminal cases.
synonymous	has the same meaning, a synonym	At times, the word court is **synonymous** with judge.

11. Evaluation, Description

Noun	Verb	Adjective	Adverb	Definition	Example
abbreviation	abbreviate	**abbreviated**		adj. short, shortened, not full length, not everything	I have given you a very **abbreviated** outline of the federal court system.
	deem			v. consider, decide, believe	The Supreme Court only chooses cases it **deems** important.
diversity	diversify	diverse diversified	diversely	n. difference, many different kinds	**Diversity** of citizenship means that the people involved in the lawsuit are from two different states.
evaluation	**evaluate**	evaluative		v. decide if something is good or bad	The jury can **evaluate** the witnesses' credibility.
equity		equitable	equitably	n. fairness, equality	**Equity** cases involve suing for some remedy other than money.
		fresh ✔		adj. recent in the mind, happened just a short time ago	A deposition allows testimony to be obtained while it is **fresh** in the witnesses' minds.
inadequacy		**inadequate** ✄	inadequately	adj. not adequate, not enough, too little	The plaintiff may allege that the damages awarded were **inadequate**.

Noun	Verb	Adjective	Adverb	Definition	Example
		nonmonetary ✂		adj. not for money, not money	Suing for **nonmonetary** remedy means no money is involved.
sufficiency	suffice	**sufficient**	sufficiently	adj. just enough, not too little, not too much	If the summons is delivered to her place of residence, then that is **sufficient** notice.
variety	vary	**various** varied	variously	adj. several different kinds	The word court has **various** meanings.

174

Appendix 1

ALADIN Blank Dictionary

Instructions: Use these blank dictionary pages to keep track of the new
academic vocabulary you learn in other classes.

1. Thinking

Noun	Verb	Adjective	Adverb	Definition	Example

1. Thinking

Noun	Verb	Adjective	Adverb	Definition	Example

2. Person Characteristics

Noun	Verb	Adjective	Adverb	Definition	Example

2. Person Characteristics

Noun	Verb	Adjective	Adverb	Definition	Example

3. Importance

Noun	Verb	Adjective	Adverb	Definition	Example

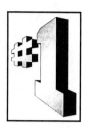

3. Importance

Noun	Verb	Adjective	Adverb	Definition	Example

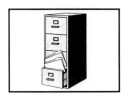

4. Information

Noun	Verb	Adjective	Adverb	Definition	Example

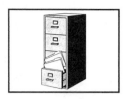

4. Information

Noun	Verb	Adjective	Adverb	Definition	Example

5. Research, Academic

Noun	Verb	Adjective	Adverb	Definition	Example

5. Research, Academic

Noun	Verb	Adjective	Adverb	Definition	Example

6. Cause-Effect, Change

Noun	Verb	Adjective	Adverb	Definition	Example

6. Cause-Effect, Change

Noun	Verb	Adjective	Adverb	Definition	Example

7. Hedge, Qualify

Hedge Word or Phrase, Qualifier	Explanation	Example

7. Hedge, Qualify

Hedge Word or Phrase, Qualifier	Explanation	Example

8. History, Government, Society

Noun	Verb	Adjective	Adverb	Definition	Example

8. History, Government, Society

Noun	Verb	Adjective	Adverb	Definition	Example

9. Time

Noun	Verb	Adjective	Adverb	Definition	Example

9. Time

Noun	Verb	Adjective	Adverb	Definition	Example

10.   Connectors and Comparisons

Connector	Meaning and Use	Example

10. Connectors and Comparisons

Connector	Meaning and Use	Example

11. Evaluation, Description

Noun	Verb	Adjective	Adverb	Definition	Example

11. Evaluation, Description

Noun	Verb	Adjective	Adverb	Definition	Example

Appendix 2

ALADIN Pretest

Instructions: Carefully tear out the Pretest pages and staple them together at the top left corner. Be sure to keep them in the right order.

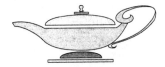

Academic Language: Assessment and Development of Individual Needs

ALADIN

Pretest 1

Name _____ Age_____ Sex ___ Year in School _____

School _____ Instructor _____ Class_____ Date _____

Race/ethnicity _____ Languages spoken at home _____

What languages do your parents speak? _____

What languages <u>other than</u> English
do you **read and write**?   **How well?**

_____   ___excellent ___good ___average ___fair ___poor
_____   ___excellent ___good ___average ___fair ___poor

‣   Do you plan to go to college? _____

‣   How many years of education are you planning to have after high school?_____
‣
‣   What job/profession do you want when you complete your education?_____

‣   How good are your **English** skills **for college work**?

My **reading** is   ___excellent ___good ___average ___below average ___poor.
My **writing** is   ___excellent ___good ___average ___below average ___poor.
My **listening** is   ___excellent ___good ___average ___below average ___poor.
My **speaking** is   ___excellent ___good ___average ___below average ___poor.

Lecture Note-taking PRETEST

Directions: Use the following two pages to take notes from the lecture. The lecture is about 11 minutes long. You will use the information in your notes to answer a question later (part 5).

_____

_____

_____

_____

_____

_____

_____

_____

_____

_____

_____

_____

_____

_____

_____

_____

_____

_____

_____

_____

_____

_____

Continue Taking Notes on The Next Page

_____ 1
_____
_____
_____
_____
_____
_____
_____
_____
_____

STOP. TURN PAGE AND GO ON TO PART 2.

Score: Writing _____   Content _____   5

Lecture Question - PRETEST

Directions: Use your lecture notes (# 1) to answer the following question about the lecture.   USE COMPLETE SENTENCES FOR YOUR ANSWER

What was the unconditioned response in Pavlov's experiment?
Why was it called unconditioned?

_____
_____
_____
_____
_____
_____
_____
_____
_____
_____

Name: _____
Endings ____/75
Vocabulary ____/90

Dictation - PRETEST

Directions: Listen to each sentence and write it down just as you hear it.

Sentence 1.

_____

_____

Sentence 2.

_____

_____

Sentence 3.

_____

_____

Sentence 4.

_____

_____

Sentence 5.

_____

_____

Sentence 6.

_____

_____

_____

Name: _____   Score: _____/32

Reading Sentence Completion Exercise - PRETEST

Directions: In each box you will find four words to choose from. Underline or circle the
word in each box that makes the sentence correct.

Example: Pavlov

| used |
| using |
| useful |
| use |

dogs in his research.

Pavlov, a Russian physiologist who

| living |
| lived |
| live |
| lives |

from 1849-1936,

| was |
| knew |
| was knowing |
| was known |

as quite a

| successful |
| successfully |
| success |
| successes |

medical scientist, but as a

| theory |
| theoretical |
| theorist |
| theorize |

he was not

| near |
| nearly |
| nearness |
| nearer |

as famous. His

| theories |
| theory |
| theorist |
| theoretical |

about the relationship between physiology and mental illness were not

| wide |
| wider |
| widely |
| widest |

accepted by

the other

| researcher |
| researching |
| researches |
| researchers |

of his day. They were just not

| interesting |
| interested |
| interest |
| interests |

in Pavlov's many

| suggests |
| suggestion |
| suggestions |
| suggested |

about mental illness. Despite his

| dependence |
| depended |
| depend |
| dependably |

on money from the government

| does |
| did |
| is doing |
| to do |

his

research and pay his

| employers |
| employees |
| employment |
| employability |

, Pavlov proved to be very out-spoken against the Communist party,

which he often

| public |
| publicizes |
| publicly |
| publicity |

denounced.   ➜ GO ON TO NEXT PAGE

[He has / Had he / He had / Has he] supported the Communists more, perhaps he [would have / wouldn't have / will have / won't have] received more money to

do his work. Such a government expected [uniformed / uniforms / uniformity / uniform] behavior from [it / it's / its / its'] citizens and did not generally

support people who, like Pavlov, [was disagreeing / is disagreeing / were disagreeing / disagrees] with the government policies. Pavlov, [be / being / was / is] a

young scientist when he met his wife, had little money. [He is / It is / They are / You are] reported that when they first got

married, they [force / forced / were forcing / were forced] to live apart because they had no money. Later, however, they led a

[tradition / traditions / traditionally / traditional] married life. Pavlov attributed much of his [professions / professional / professionally / profession] success to his wife, [whose / whom / who / who's]

life was [devoted / devoting / devote / devotes] to taking care of her husband and [supported / supports / supporting / support] his work. In his personal habits Pavlov

was quite [predictable / predicted / predicting / predictably] and [arrived / arrives / arrive / arriving] on time in the laboratory even when there [was / is / were / are] rioting

[takes / taken / taking / took] place on the streets outside. Pavlov's [accomplishment / accomplishing / accomplished / accomplishments] were honored by his country and the

world when he was awarded the Nobel Prize for physiology in 1904.

DIRECTIONS: Circle the number that shows how well you know each word below.	1 I don't recognize this word.	2 I've **seen** this word before but I don't know what it means.	3 I **think** I know what this word means but I am not 100% sure.	4 I know what this word means and I can **probably** use it in a sentence.	5 I know this word and I have used it recently in speaking or writing.
1. identical	1	2	3	4	5
2. culture	1	2	3	4	5
3. assumption	1	2	3	4	5
4. predictable	1	2	3	4	5
5. experimental	1	2	3	4	5
6. capacity	1	2	3	4	5
7. hence	1	2	3	4	5
8. significant	1	2	3	4	5
9. consequences	1	2	3	4	5
10. probability	1	2	3	4	5
11. specifically	1	2	3	4	5
12. verification	1	2	3	4	5
13. demonstrate	1	2	3	4	5
14. reluctance	1	2	3	4	5
15. emphasis	1	2	3	4	5
16. trend	1	2	3	4	5
17. explicit	1	2	3	4	5
18. ambiguity	1	2	3	4	5
19. inference	1	2	3	4	5
20. derivation	1	2	3	4	5
21. socioeconomic	1	2	3	4	5
22. speculate	1	2	3	4	5
23. notwithstanding	1	2	3	4	5
24. arbitrary	1	2	3	4	5
25. empirical	1	2	3	4	5

GO BACK TO PART 5

Directions: Underline the important information as you read the <u>whole</u> page.

LEARNING

Conditioning is one form of learning. Learning is the acquisition of information and knowledge, of skills and habits, and of attitudes and beliefs. It always involves a change in one of these areas--a change that is brought about by the learner's experiences. Accordingly, psychologists define learning as all changes in behavior that result from experience, providing these changes are relatively permanent, do not result simply from growth or maturation, and are not the temporary effects of factors such as fatigue or drugs. Drug abuse was a big problem especially in the 1960s.

Change is interesting. Not all changes involved in learning are obvious and observable. For example, learning often involves changes in the learner's disposition--that is, in the person's inclination to do or not to do something. Hence changes in disposition have to do with motivation. Such changes cannot always be observed by teachers and others but are no less real or important.

Learning involves not only changes in disposition, but also changes in capability--that is, changes in the skills or knowledge required to do something (Gagne, 1985). Like changes in disposition, changes in capability cannot always be observed directly. To determine whether or not students' dispositions or capabilities have changed following instruction, teachers must provide them with an opportunity to engage in the relevant behavior. In most countries, teachers do not earn very much money. If instruction affects learners in such a way that their behaviors after instruction are observably different from those before instruction, we can conclude that learning has occurred. Even adults continue to learn all their lives.

BEHAVIORISM AND COGNITIVISM

Two major groups of theories relate to learning: behaviorism and cognitivism. Later you will read about several minor theories. Differences between these two major groups of learning theories center mainly on the questions each tries to answer. Behaviorism tries to explain simple behaviors--observable and predictable responses. Accordingly, it is concerned mainly with conditions (called stimuli) that affect organisms and that may lead to behavior, as well as with simple behaviors themselves (responses).

Behavior-oriented (or behavioristic) researchers attempt to discover the rules that govern the formation of relationships between stimuli and responses (the rules of conditioning). For this reason, behavioristic theories are often referred to as stimulus-response (S-R) theories. Researchers often use just one letter or symbol (such as S-R) to represent a word or concept.

In contrast to behaviorism, cognitive approaches deal primarily with questions relating to cognition, or knowing. Cognitive theorists are concerned with how we develop a fund of knowledge. Knowledge is power. Cognition-oriented researchers attempt to understand the nature of information--how it is acquired and organized by learners; how it can be recalled, modified, applied, and analyzed; and how the learner understands, evaluates, and controls the activities involved in cognition (metacognition).

COGNITIVISM

In a behavioristic analysis of learning, the primary emphasis is on the external conditions that affect behavior. In contrast to behaviorism, cognitivism involves the scientific study of mental events (E. Gagne, 1985, p. 4). Gagne was a professor at University of Iowa in the 1970s. Mental events have to do with acquiring, processing, storing, and retrieving information. Computers also process, store, and retrieve information. The primary emphasis in a cognitive analysis of learning is on the learner's mental structure, a concept that includes not only the learner's previous related knowledge, but also the strategies that the learner might bring to bear on the present situation. In this view, the explicit assumption is that learners are far from equal. It is the individual's preexisting network of concepts, strategies, and understanding that makes experience meaningful. Although learners may not be equal in the classroom, they are considered equal in a democracy.

Cognitivism focuses on knowledge; hence cognition is knowing. Cognition is a word used often in psychology books. One of the major emphases of cognitive approaches concerns the ways information is processed and stored. This departs dramatically from the major emphasis of a behavioristic approach, which involves behavior and its consequences.

Name _____

Score:

Content/Verbatim _____

7

Reading Summary - PRETEST

Directions: Use the space below to summarize the important information in the paragraph that is contained in the box surrounded by dotted lines. Do not try to summarize the whole reading page. Summarize means to write several sentences that present the important information. Be sure to organize your writing and use <u>complete sentences</u> in your answer. Use your own words as much as possible to write the summary. Do not just copy sentences from the reading passage.

Summary of Reading in the Box

_____

_____

_____

_____

_____

_____

_____

_____

_____

_____

_____

_____

_____

_____

_____

_____

_____

Name: _____

Now that the test is finished and you have had a chance to practice these language skills, answer the following question again:

How good are your English skills **for college work**? (check one)

My **reading** ability is	___excellent	___good	___average	___below average	___poor.
My **writing** ability is	___excellent	___good	___average	___below average	___poor.
My **listening** ability is	___excellent	___good	___average	___below average	___poor.
My **speaking** ability is	___excellent	___good	___average	___below average	___poor.

Appendix 3

ALADIN Posttest

Instructions: Carefully tear out the Posttest pages and staple them
together at the top left corner. Be sure to keep them in the
right order.

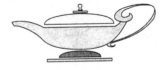

Academic Language: Assessment and Development of Individual Needs

ALADIN

Posttest 1

Name _____ Age_____ Sex ___ Year in School _____

School _____ Instructor _____ Class_____ Date_____

Race/ethnicity _____ Languages spoken at home _____

What languages do your parents speak? _____

What languages <u>other than</u> English
do you **read and write**?   **How well?**

_____   ___excellent ___good ___average ___fair ___poor
_____   ___excellent ___good ___average ___fair ___poor

▸   Do you plan to go to college? _____

▸   How many years of education are you planning to have after high school?_____

▸
▸   What job/profession do you want when you complete your education?_____

▸   How good are your **English** skills **for college work**?

My **reading** is	___excellent	___good	___average	___below average ___poor.
My **writing** is	___excellent	___good	___average	___below average ___poor.
My **listening** is	___excellent	___good	___average	___below average ___poor.
My **speaking** is	___excellent	___good	___average	___below average ___poor.

Lecture Note-taking POSTTEST

Directions: Use the following two pages to take notes from the lecture. The lecture is about 11 minutes long. You will use the information in your notes to answer a question later (part 5).

_____

_____

_____

_____

_____

_____

_____

_____

_____

_____

_____

_____

_____

_____

_____

_____

_____

_____

_____

_____

_____

_____

_____

Continue Taking Notes on The Next Page

_____ 1
_____
_____
_____
_____
_____
_____
_____
_____
_____

STOP   TURN PAGE AND GO ON TO PART 2.

Score: Writing _____   Content _____   5

Lecture Question - POSTTEST

Directions: Use your lecture notes (# 1) to answer the following question about the lecture. USE COMPLETE SENTENCES FOR YOUR ANSWER

Skinner said that there are no universal reinforcers. Explain what a reinforcer is.

_____
_____
_____
_____
_____
_____
_____
_____
_____
_____

Score:
Endings ____/75
Vocabulary ____/90

Name: _____

Dictation - POSTTEST

Directions: Listen to each sentence and write it down just as you hear it.

Sentence 1.

_____

_____

Sentence 2.

_____

_____

Sentence 3.

_____

_____

Sentence 4.

_____

_____

Sentence 5.

_____

_____

Sentence 6.

_____

_____

_____

Reading Sentence Completion Exercise - POSTTEST

Directions: In each box you will find four words to choose from. Underline or circle
the word in each box that makes the sentence correct.

Example: Skinner | will become
<u>became</u>
becomes
is becoming | a professor in 1939.

B.F. Skinner, a famous | behavior
behaviorism
behaviorist
behaviors | , received his Ph.D. from Harvard University in 1931. He

was one of the most | influences
influenced
influentially
influential | psychologists of the | twentieth
twenty
twenties
twentyish | century. Skinner was

| great
greatly
greater
greatest | influenced by both Pavlov and Thorndike, | who
whom
whose
who's | theories he expanded upon.

Like | your
their
our
his | predecessors, Skinner studied the behavior of animals in order to understand

human | learned
learning
learns
learner | . Although Skinner | using
uses
use
used | pigeons in his research, he tried to | generalizes
generalize
generalized
generalizable |

their behavior to | humans
humanizes
humanist
human | just as the earlier behaviorists | do
are doing
has done
had done | . During World War II,

Skinner's | trained
trains
training
trainer | of pigeons to pilot   **➔ GO ON TO NEXT PAGE**

torpedoes and bombs [are / were / was / is] part of the war [research / researchers / researches / researched] effort. The [plan / planning / planned / plans] use of 3

the birds as missile guides, however, was never [implemented / implementing / implements / implement] . Skinner gained some

[measurable / measure / measuring / measured] [publicly / publicize / publics / public] of attention through the [invented / invent / invention / invents] of his Air-Crib. This was a large,

soundproof, germ-free, air-conditioned box [designed / designs / designing / design] to serve as a [mechanic / mechanical / mechanics / mechanically] babysitter.

Skinner believed that this box provided an [optimums / optimally / optimal / optimize] environment for child [growth / to grow / grown / grew] during the

first two years of life. [Usefully / Used / Using / Use] various kinds of [experimental / experimentally / experiments / experimented] equipment that he invented, he

trained pigeons to perform quite [except / exceptional / exceptionally / excepted] actions. For example, he trained pigeons [play / played / player / to play]

ping-pong. One of Skinner's famous inventions is [used / usefully / using / useful] by drug companies to observe how a

drug may [modifying / modifies / modify / modifiable] animal behavior. The step-by-step [trained / training / train / trainer] of research animals [lead / leading / leads / led]

Skinner to the principles of programmed learning through the use of [teaching / teaches / teach / teachers] machines.

DIRECTIONS: Circle the number that shows how well you know each word below.	1 I don't recognize this word.	2 I've **seen** this word before but I don't know what it means.	3 I **think** I know what this word means but I am not 100% sure.	4 I know what this word means and I can **probably** use it in a sentence.	5 I know this word and I have used it recently in speaking or writing.
1. primarily	1	2	3	4	5
2. acquire	1	2	3	4	5
3. assumption	1	2	3	4	5
4. overwhelmingly	1	2	3	4	5
5. significant	1	2	3	4	5
6. external	1	2	3	4	5
7. capacity	1	2	3	4	5
8. ongoing	1	2	3	4	5
9. consciousness	1	2	3	4	5
10. retrieve	1	2	3	4	5
11. passive	1	2	3	4	5
12. portrays	1	2	3	4	5
13. undergoes	1	2	3	4	5
14. essence	1	2	3	4	5
15. superficial	1	2	3	4	5
16. trivial	1	2	3	4	5
17. fleeting	1	2	3	4	5
18. speculate	1	2	3	4	5
19. conceptual	1	2	3	4	5
20. bulk	1	2	3	4	5
21. transference	1	2	3	4	5
22. accordingly	1	2	3	4	5
23. physical	1	2	3	4	5
24. synthesizing	1	2	3	4	5
25. distinctive	1	2	3	4	5

GO BACK TO PART 5

Directions: Underline the important information as you read the <u>whole</u> page.

A BASIC INFORMATION-PROCESSING MODEL

The widely-accepted basic model portrays the human information processor in terms of three types of information storage: short-term sensory storage, short-term memory, and long-term memory. These are the three types of storage. Each type of storage is distinct from the others primarily in terms of the nature and extent of the processing that information undergoes. Processing refers to activities such as organizing, analyzing, synthesizing, rehearsing, and so on. Models are important.

The information-processing model attempts to represent how we acquire information, how we sort and organize it, and how we later retrieve it. The model is, in effect, a learning and memory model that begins with the raw material of all learning experiences: sensory input. Input is not the same as output.

SENSORY MEMORY: Our sensory systems (vision, hearing, taste, touch, smell) are sensitive to an overwhelmingly wide range of stimulation. In fact, some things smell bad. Clearly, however, they respond only to a fraction of all available stimulation at any given time; the bulk of the information available in this stimulation is never actually processed--that is, it never actually becomes part of our cognitive structure. The label sensory memory refers to the fleeting (less than one second) and unconscious effect on us of stimulation to which we pay no attention. Less than one second is very little time. Sensory memory is highly limited, not only in terms of the length of time during which stimulus information is available for processing, but also in terms of the absolute amount of information available.

SHORT-TERM MEMORY: The information-processing system of which cognitive psychology speaks makes use of a number of different activities with a common goal: making sense of significant sensory input and, at the same time, ignoring or discarding more trivial input. A great deal of sensory input that is not attended to does not go beyond immediate sensory memory. Paying attention is, in fact, one of the important activities of our information-processing system. It is the means by which input is transferred from sensory to short-term storage. Be sure to pay attention!

In essence, short-term memory consists of what is in our immediate consciousness at any given time. For this reason, short-term memory is often called working memory.

One of the important characteristics of short-term memory is that it is highly limited in capacity. Following various memory experiments, Miller (1956) concluded that its average capacity is around seven discrete items (plus or minus two); that is, our immediate conscious awareness is limited to this capacity, and as additional items of information come in, they push out some that are already there.

LONG-TERM MEMORY

The type of memory that is clearly of greatest concern to educators is long-term memory. Long-term memory includes all of our relatively stable information about the world--all that we know but that is not in our immediate consciousness. In fact, one of the important distinctions between short-term and long-term memory is that short-term memory is an active, ongoing, conscious process, whereas long-term memory is a more passive, unconscious process. Accordingly, short-term memory is easily disrupted by external events--as we demonstrate when we lose our "train of thought" due to some distraction. In contrast, long-term memory cannot easily be disrupted.

The transference of material from short-term to long-term memory involves more than simple rehearsal: It involves encoding, a process whereby meaning is derived from experience. To encode information involves information processing, an event that can occur at different levels. Not all material in long-term memory is processed to the same level. If subjects are asked to learn and remember a word, they can process it at a very superficial level, paying attention only to its physical appearance. At a somewhat deeper level, they might pay attention to the word's meaning, and at the deepest level, to the word's conceptual relations.

Score: Content/Verbatim _____

Reading Summary - POSTTEST

Directions: Use the space below to summarize the important information in the two paragraphs that are contained in the box surrounded by dotted lines. Do not try to summarize the whole reading page. Summarize means to write several sentences that present the important information. Be sure to organize your writing and use complete sentences in your answer. Use your own words as much as possible to write the summary. Do not just copy sentences from the reading passage.

Summary of Reading in the Box

_____

_____

_____

_____

_____

_____

_____

_____

_____

_____

_____

_____

_____

_____

_____

_____

End of Posttest